Mathematics
Programs

Essential Tools for Educators

The Program Evaluation Guides for Schools
Richard M. Jaeger, Series Editor

Evaluating School Programs: An Educator's Guide
James R. Sanders

Special Education Programs: A Guide to Evaluation
Ada L. Vallecorsa, Laurie U. deBettencourt, Elizabeth Garriss

Counseling Programs: A Guide to Evaluation
L. DiAnne Borders, Sandra M. Drury

Reading and Language Arts Programs: A Guide to Evaluation
Mary W. Olson, Samuel D. Miller

Programs for At-Risk Students: A Guide to Evaluation
Rita G. O'Sullivan, Cheryl V. Tennant

Mathematics Programs: A Guide to Evaluation
George W. Bright, A. Edward Uprichard, Janice H. Jetton

George W. Bright
A. Edward Uprichard
Janice H. Jetton

Mathematics Programs

A Guide to Evaluation

The Program Evaluation Guides for Schools
Series Editor: Richard M. Jaeger

CORWIN PRESS, INC.
A Sage Publications Company
Newbury Park, California 91320

For information address:

Corwin Press, Inc.
A Sage Publications Company
2455 Teller Road
Newbury Park, California 91320

SAGE Publications Ltd.
6 Bonhill Street
London EC2A 4PU
United Kingdom

SAGE Publications India Pvt. Ltd.
M-32 Market
Greater Kailash I
New Delhi 110 048 India

Printed in the United States of America

Library of Congress Cataloging-in-Publication Data
Bright, George W.
    Mathematics programs: a guide to evaluation / George W. Bright, A. Edward Uprichard, Janice H. Jetton.
        p. cm. — (Essential tools for educators)
    Includes bibliographical references and index.
    ISBN 0-8039-6044-1 (pbk.)
    1. Mathematics—Study and teaching—Evaluation. 2. Curriculum evaluation. I. Uprichard, A. Edward II. Jetton, Janice H.
III. Title. IV. Series.
QA11.B795 1993
371.2'913—dc20   92-37325

The paper in this book meets the specifications for permanence of the American National Standards Institute and the National Association of State Textbook Administrators.

93 94 95 96 10 9 8 7 6 5 4 3 2 1

Corwin Press Production Editor: Tara S. Mead

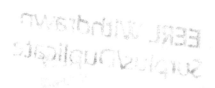

Contents

Series Editor's Preface

Essential Tools for Educators: The Program Evaluation Guides for Schools is a series grounded in the premise that regular evaluation of school programs can be of enormous help to school professionals—provided *they* are the ones who plan the evaluations, conduct the evaluations, and use the evaluations to guide their school improvement activities. Evaluation is a powerful tool for documenting school needs, identifying strengths and weaknesses in school programs, and discovering how to improve almost every aspect of school life. Program evaluation need not be complex or inordinately time-consuming. Simple principles and strategies are described in the initial volume of this series, *Evaluating School Programs: An Educator's Guide*. Then, specific techniques and approaches are illustrated in the program-focused guides that complete the series. Using these principles and techniques, teachers, principals, and other school professionals *can* plan, conduct, and interpret the findings of powerful evaluations of their curricula; of their instructional programs in mathematics, reading, language arts, and special education; of their programs for "at-risk" students; and of their counseling and personnel development programs. The principles to be learned from this series can be applied even more broadly to the evaluation of school disciplinary programs, student assessment programs, community relations programs, and other programmatic elements that are central to the successful functioning of a school.

Extensive technical training is *not* prerequisite to planning and conducting sound evaluations of school programs. Sound evaluation *does* require a desire to improve one's school, willingness to work collegially, careful attention to detail, and basic knowledge of how school program evaluations should be carried out. The ETE series provides school professionals with the last of these elements—the essential tools they need to plan and conduct effective evaluations of their school programs.

Evaluating School Programs: An Educator's Guide is the foundation volume in this series. It contains a clear, concise exposition of the objectives, principles, and core issues that undergird solid evaluations of school programs. By reading this guide, teachers, principals, and their colleagues will learn how to (a) determine the feasibility of conducting a school program evaluation, (b) focus a school program evaluation, (c) structure and design a school program evaluation, (d) conduct a school program evaluation, (e) interpret the results of a school program evaluation, (f) report and make use of the results of a school program evaluation, and (g) ensure that a school program evaluation is conducted ethically, damages no one, and enriches all who are associated with the program being evaluated.

Once these basic elements of a school evaluation are well understood, readers will be ready to proceed to the guide in this series that focuses on the subject area of the program to be evaluated. Each program-specific guide provides specific instruction on the evaluation of school programs in a single subject area, and each follows a consistent pattern of organization. Following an introduction that provides an overview and rationale for program evaluation in its subject area, each program-specific guide contains a sequence of vignettes (chapters) that illustrate, in detail, evaluation of a focused aspect of a school program. Collectively, these vignettes illustrate how evaluations of school programs are planned, structured, staffed, conducted, interpreted, and used. The vignettes cover a wide range of practical evaluative issues; illustrate the selection, development, and use of a large number of evaluation strategies and instruments; and show how the results of evaluation can be used to strengthen school programs. Resources at the end of each program-specific guide contain a set of research-based standards and indicators of school program quality, a road map to the use of these standards in evaluating the effectiveness and efficiency of a school program, and an annotated bibliography of selected references on program evaluation in the subject area of the guide.

Evaluations can help school professionals make their school the best it can be and, in the process, substantially increase their own educational effectiveness. In the hands of thoughtful, well-trained school professionals, evaluation can be a transformative catalyst that improves schools and all who work and learn in them. The ETE series will help you become one of those distinctive school professionals who can make school program evaluations work well. Knowing that your investment in this knowledge will pay rich dividends for years to come, I wish you every success.

RICHARD M. JAEGER
University of North Carolina,
Greensboro

About the Authors

George W. Bright is Professor of Mathematics Education at the University of North Carolina at Greensboro, where he teaches research, curriculum, and methods courses to graduate and undergraduate students. He has directed a variety of inservice, research, and curriculum development projects across kindergarten through Grade 12. His current scholarly interests include the use of technology in teaching mathematics, the infusion of statistics content throughout the mathematics curriculum, and evaluation of mathematics education inservice programs. He has published more than 100 articles in professional journals, and he is author or coauthor of more than a dozen books, including *Learning and Mathematics Games, Microcomputer Applications in the Elementary Classroom: A Guide for Teachers,* and *Essential Computing Skills for Teachers.* He has served as editor of *Focus on Learning Problems in Mathematics,* the official journal of the Research Council for Diagnostic and Prescriptive Mathematics, and he is associate editor of *Journal of Technology in Mathematics.* In 1992, he received an award from the Society for Technology and Teacher Education for outstanding research on classroom behavior of teachers. He has served on several committees of national and regional professional organizations and as regional vice-president of the Honor Society of Phi Kappa Phi. He holds a Ph.D. (1971) in mathematics education from the University of Texas at Austin and an M.A. (1969) and B.A., magna cum laude (1968), in mathematics from William Marsh Rice University. He is a member of Phi Beta Kappa.

A. Edward Uprichard is Professor of Mathematics Education and Dean of the School of Education at the University of North Carolina at Greensboro. Before coming to North Carolina, he served as a faculty member and an administrator (department chairperson and Associate Dean) in the College of Education at the University of South Florida, from 1969 to 1988, where he taught a variety of mathematics education courses to undergraduate and graduate students in elementary education, mathematics education, and special education, and provided extensive inservice work for elementary school and middle school teachers from throughout Florida and the Southeast. His research interests relate to mathematics problem solving, diagnosing mathematical difficulties, and paradigms for studying mathematics learning. He has cowritten two books, *Fundamentals Underlying Number* and *Diagnosing Mathematical Difficulties,* written more than 80 scholarly articles and papers, and served as editor of *Focus on Learning Problems in Mathematics,* the official journal of the Research Council for Diagnostic and Prescriptive Mathematics. He is a member of several professional organizations such as the National Council of Teachers of Mathematics, the American Educational Research Association, and the Association of Teacher Educators. His experience as an elementary school teacher in New York has enhanced his work as a mathematics educator. He holds a Ph.D. (1969) and an M.S. (1966) in Mathematics Education from Syracuse University and a B.A. in Elementary Education with emphases in mathematics and music from the State University of New York at Fredonia.

Janice H. Jetton holds a B.S., an M.A., and a certificate of advanced study from Appalachian State University (ASU) and an Ed.D. in curriculum and teaching from the University of North Carolina at Greensboro. She has been employed as a secondary mathematics teacher in Caldwell County Schools, North Carolina, for the past 21 years. She has been an adjunct faculty member of ASU since 1977, serving as the Admissions Partnership Program mathematics instructor. She teaches problem-solving strategies as part of the Summer Ventures program in science and mathematics. In addition to her other responsibilities, she is employed as a Lecturer in the Department of Mathematical Sciences on the ASU campus. She is a member of several professional organizations, including the North Carolina Association of Educators, National Education Association, North Carolina Council for Teachers of Mathematics, National Council of Teachers of Mathematics, and the Association of Supervision and Curriculum. She has been listed in the second edition of *Who's Who Among America's Teachers.*

Introduction

What Is the Purpose of This Guide?

Improving Instructional Programs With Ongoing Evaluations

This guide has been written to assist teachers of mathematics in kindergarten through Grade 12 and other school personnel who are responsible for or interested in designing and conducting evaluations of mathematics programs at the school or district level where the emphasis is on improvement of programs, securing needed resources, and helping professionals work together more effectively. The philosophy underlying this guide is that school personnel (teachers, administrators, specialty teachers, and so on) can improve instructional programs in their schools by examining their quality in a systematic or ongoing way, using criteria that have been found to characterize effective and successful content-specific programs. The focus is on evaluations conducted by school personnel on their own terms and for their own purposes rather than on mandates imposed by others.

This guide was not written with expert evaluators in mind. While program evaluations must be thoughtfully and carefully planned to produce trustworthy or valid results, they need not involve sophisticated statistical procedures or fancy research techniques. It is believed that, by reading this guide and the accompanying *Evaluating School Programs: An Educator's Guide,* teachers of mathematics can develop the knowledge and skills to plan and conduct useful evaluations.

Why Evaluate the Mathematics Program?

There are many reasons for evaluating a mathematics program, for example, low test scores, declining enrollments in some courses, increasing lethargy of the faculty, and so on. Each of the scenarios that follow illustrates a reason for evaluating a mathematics program.

Teachers Seek Additional Resources

Scenario 1. At the end of last year, Mr. Brown, principal of Bennett Elementary, had several teachers approach him to discuss the possibility of acquiring a mathematics computer laboratory. Although they were able to convince Mr. Brown of the need for such a laboratory, which would be shared by all grade levels on periodic days during mathematics time, Mr. Brown warned his faculty that receiving funding from the school board would be difficult. All agreed that the best way to ensure school board funding for a new laboratory was to develop a proposal that would include documentation of the effective use of all resource material currently accessible to the mathematics program at Bennett Elementary.

Department Chair's Alarm About Decline in Enrollment

Scenario 2. During the past 5 years, the mathematics faculty at Greene High School has seen a slow but steady decline in course enrollment figures, especially among junior and senior students. With fewer than 5% of the typical senior class enrolled in advanced levels of mathematics appropriate for 12th-grade students, Mr. Black, the mathematics chairperson, is alarmed. He has called a special meeting for the mathematics teachers, counselors, and the principal to discuss the situation. Mr. Black hopes that the group can work together to study the problem and to identify some action steps to correct it.

Principal's Concern About Test Scores

Scenario 3. Mrs. Sams has been dissatisfied with test scores at Smith High School since she became principal. Her top priority is to see that Smith's SAT scores, achievement test scores, and the end-of-course test scores become more competitive with and surpass the county and state averages. Her analysis of students' test scores over the past 2 years indicated that students were experiencing difficulty with mathematics, especially problem solving. Mrs. Sams shared her analysis with the mathematics teachers at Smith and asked them to develop a plan to determine the quality of the mathematics curriculum.

Superintendent's Interest in Equal Access to Instruction

Scenario 4. The Hastings School Board is very concerned that all students have equal access to appropriate mathematics instruction. Teachers from across the school district claim that this is not the case, especially at the middle school, where an increasing number of course options, and resulting tracking of students based on test scores, seems to be developing in the seventh and eighth grades. The superintendent is interested in determining whether the teachers' claims are valid.

In each of these scenarios, information is needed by school personnel to answer a question or to address a concern. Ongoing evaluations of mathematics programs can be useful in many situations. The following reasons suggest situations for which an evaluation would be needed:

Reasons for Evaluating Mathematics Programs

- to set priorities among needs and to translate needs into a mathematics program that has relevance to a particular school and student body
- to determine the adequacy of current resources to implement a particular mathematics program or to establish the need for additional resources
- to determine the effectiveness of an existing mathematics program or program components to see if changes are needed

    For example, what is the nature of the current program as delivered? Do program components operate in intended ways? What program strengths can be used to greater effect? What program weaknesses should be remedied?

- to determine whether a mathematics program or program components should be discontinued
- to determine whether a mathematics program meets standards set by a professional organization

    For example, the National Council of Teachers of Mathematics (NCTM) has published *Curriculum and Evaluation Standards for School Mathematics* (1989).

Evaluation Is a Tool for School Personnel

Results from a mathematics program evaluation can be used to facilitate meaningful dialogue between/among teachers, administrators, school board members, and the local community and beyond. Sound program evaluation can help school personnel make mathematics programs better as well as gain political support and resources for programs. In brief, program evaluation is a tool for school personnel!

What Is in This Guide?

The Educator's Guide and Companion Guides

This guide is part of a series. The first guide in the series, *Evaluating School Programs: An Educator's Guide,* describes the steps in conducting a program evaluation, including ways to focus an evaluation, to identify specific evaluation questions, to collect information, and then to organize, analyze, and report the information. Companion guides, addressing specific school programs such as mathematics, reading and language arts, and school guidance and counseling, illustrate in depth the steps presented in the *Educator's Guide.* The *Educator's Guide* should be read before any of the companion guides. The program-specific guides are not comprehensive texts on program evaluation; they stand together with the *Educator's Guide* to provide assistance for school personnel in their evaluation efforts.

Standards and Indicators: Characteristics of Effective Programs

The first step in preparing this guide was to do an extensive review of the literature related to school mathematics content, the teaching of mathematics, and assessment. Close attention was given to the National Council of Teachers of Mathematics' *Curriculum and Evaluation Standards for School Mathematics* (1989) and the *Professional Standards for Teaching Mathematics* (1991). The literature review was then used to create the list of characteristics (standards and indicators) of effective school mathematics programs that appears in Resource A. This list can be used in thinking about the qualities and characteristics of a program and in deciding what components or aspects of a program should be evaluated.

Vignettes: Planning, Designing, and Conducting an Evaluation

This mathematics guide consists of a series of vignettes containing miniature case studies. Although the vignettes deal with some of the same issues as the scenarios presented earlier, they do not strictly parallel one another. Each vignette illustrates the planning, designing, and conducting of a mathematics program evaluation as an orderly sequence of steps using the principles articulated in the *Educator's Guide* and is based on a standard and indicator(s) listed in Resource A. In each vignette, the school setting and the focus of the evaluation are described. Also described are the mathematics teachers' deliberations concerning the choice of an evaluation strategy that will provide information that is directly related to the focus of the evaluation and the use of the selected evaluation strategy. Data collection, analysis, and interpretation (application of the results) are illustrated, and implications for the program are discussed. Finally, a list of the evaluation principles illustrated in the vignette, alternative evaluation strategies that could have been used, and some precautions regarding misinterpretations of the evaluation results are presented.

Evaluation Strategies Associated With Indicators

Evaluations of elementary school, middle school, and high school mathematics programs are included in the vignettes. While the evaluations are school specific, the evaluation strategies described in each vignette can be used in most school settings. For each of the indicators listed in Resource A, associated evaluation strategies are suggested, and some reference one or more vignettes that illustrate the use of those strategies.

In preparing this guide, several decisions had to be made about which mathematics standards and indicators to include in the vignettes. Because the standards and indicators listed in Resource A covered different areas of concern—content, teaching, and assessment—it was decided to include at least one from each of the three areas.

Further, standards and indicators were selected based on their potential appeal to a broad range of teachers of mathematics and other school personnel. Selection was also influenced by our goals of illustrating a variety of data collection procedures and methods for organizing, analyzing, and reporting results.

How Do I Use This Guide?

Steps in Using This Guide

First, read the *Educator's Guide* to learn the basics of planning, designing, and conducting an evaluation. Next, skim this mathematics guide, especially the vignettes and Resource A, to get an overview of its contents and an orientation to the types of mathematics program evaluations that can be conducted. When you are ready to plan your own evaluation, the following sequence of steps is suggested.

Proactive or Systematic Evaluation

Focus the evaluation. (See Chapter 2 in the *Educator's Guide.*) Program evaluations are conducted to answer a particular question(s) or address a specific concern(s). An evaluation can be based on priorities set in a school improvement plan (proactive) or on external influences such as a legislative mandate (reactive). Proactive or systematic evaluations tend to be more effective in improving school programs than those conducted in response to a mandate. In any case, thoughtful planning is necessary to focus an evaluation so that the results will provide relevant and valid information. Reviewing the list of standards and indicators in Resource A can help stimulate ideas and help focus an evaluation; the questions below can help teachers of mathematics and others to focus an evaluation or decide what to evaluate.

Purpose: Needs Assessment, Formative Evaluation, or Summative Evaluation

(1) Why is the mathematics program being evaluated? Evaluations can be conducted to assess students' needs, to assess program goals, to improve program design, to improve program operation, to improve program effectiveness, to improve program efficiency, and so on. The purpose of an evaluation will obviously influence the evaluation plan. Different purposes lead to different sets of expectations that need to be understood and addressed. For example, will the evaluation take the form of a needs assessment, a formative evaluation, or a summative evaluation? Needs assessment data are used to set priorities and establish program goals. Formative evaluation data are collected while the program is being implemented and the data are used to make decisions about "midcourse corrections" that will improve the program. Summative evaluation data are collected at the completion of a program and the data are used to determine whether

a program will be continued. Some specifics related to the purpose include the following:

> Who is initiating the evaluation? Is the evaluation being conducted for your own reasons, or are you responding to a request from someone else?
>
> Who will have access to the results?
>
> What will you and/or others do with the results?
>
> What decisions will be based on the results?
>
> What actions might be taken based on the results?

Focus   *(2) Which components of the mathematics program should be evaluated?* This question is related to the purpose. Which program components are most relevant to the intended decisions or actions? What standards or indicators are most critical to the decisions or actions? The intention of the evaluation—decisions or actions that will be based on the evaluation results—identify which program components are to be evaluated. The focus of a program evaluation might be determined by an evaluator or evaluation team based on priorities set in a school improvement plan.

Time, Talent,   *(3) What resources are available?* Resources include time, talent,
and Money   and money. Who will coordinate the evaluation? Who will work on the evaluation? How much time will be available to persons who work on the evaluation? Do the persons working on the evaluation have all the required skills? If not, who else must be involved? Are the funds necessary to support the evaluation available? Clearly, the scope of an evaluation will depend on available resources. Also, teachers of mathematics should not always assume that they can conduct a program evaluation by themselves. Some evaluations can be quite time consuming and certain projects may require the specialized skills of other school personnel or an outside consultant. A consultant may be needed to help with designing data collection instruments, producing and distributing them, and/or tallying and analyzing the results. In most cases, however, school personnel can do the job themselves.

A program evaluation plan must have a sense of purpose, a focus, and address available resources. The standards and indicators listed in Resource A characterize effective school mathematics programs and can be especially helpful in focusing an evaluation. In each vignette, the deliberations of teachers in focusing an evaluation are described. All of the questions raised in this section are important and must be addressed by careful and thoughtful planning.

Choosing an Evaluation Strategy

Collect information. (See Chapter 3 in the *Educator's Guide.*) What information is needed to answer the questions or address the concerns that have been identified, and how is that information to be collected? In each of the vignettes, teachers of mathematics consider several approaches to collecting data; advantages and disadvantages are discussed. Also, alternative approaches are discussed in a separate section within each vignette. This information can help you choose the general strategy or approach to be followed in collecting data and the specific procedures to be followed.

Resource A also can be helpful in locating information on a specific evaluation strategy. The last column in Resource A indicates which vignette(s) illustrates the evaluation strategies suggested for each indicator. Referring to the referenced vignette may be helpful in gaining information about a specific evaluation strategy and its use.

Specific questions relevant to the task of collecting information include the following:

Who will work on the evaluation? One person? An evaluation team?

Who will be the evaluation leader?

What data collection procedures will be used?

When will they be used?

Who will collect the data? Do these persons need to be trained?

If instruments (e.g., surveys, questionnaires, checklists) are to be used, how will respondents be selected?

How long will it take to collect the information?

Who will tabulate and analyze the data? Do these persons need to be trained?

How will confidentiality be maintained? Is informed consent needed?

Constructing a Timeline

Organize the evaluation. (See Chapters 3 and 4 in the *Educator's Guide.*) An effective evaluation plan is a well-organized evaluation plan. A helpful resource for organizing an evaluation plan is the construction of a timeline that specifies each task to be completed, the person(s) responsible for each task, and beginning and ending dates for the accomplishment of each task. Tasks can relate to identifying and securing resources, developing instrumentation, collecting information, analyzing information, and reporting information. A timeline is used by an evaluator or an evaluation team to monitor the evaluation as it unfolds and to make any necessary adjustments to schedules, tasks, and so on.

Qualitative Data and/or Quantitative Data

Analyze the information. (See Chapter 4 in the *Educator's Guide.*) Before any evaluation data are collected, decisions must be made about how the data will be analyzed and summarized so that the message from the evaluation data is accurate and clear. Evaluation data may be qualitative (narrative) or quantitative (numerical) or both. Qualitative data can be summarized into categories and the analysis can involve searching for patterns. Quantitative data lend themselves to frequency distributions (graphs or charts), measures of central tendency (means, median, and mode), and/or measures of the variance of scores (e.g., range, standard deviation). Various approaches to summarizing and analyzing data are illustrated in the vignettes. Mathematics teachers will need to decide who will analyze the data and whether they need any special training.

The final step before reporting the results of a program evaluation is to interpret or attach value judgments to the information now available. What does it mean for our program? What are the implications for program improvement? For change?

Keep in Mind Purpose and Audience

Report the results. (See Chapter 5 in the *Educator's Guide.*) In preparing the report of an evaluation, you will need to keep in mind the purpose of the evaluation, the major audiences (decision makers) for the results, and the best medium to communicate with different audiences. Whether or not a formal written report is required depends largely upon the audience for the evaluation. If the audience for an evaluation of a mathematics program consists solely of the school's mathematics teachers and principal, modest forms of reporting evaluation results and recommendations, such as a memo, committee report, or program plan, may be most appropriate. In any case, a report should include a clear description of the focus of the evaluation (questions to be answered or concerns addressed), a written record of the steps used to conduct the evaluation, and a written summary of the results.

The following questions might be helpful in thinking about the preparation of a final report:

> What types of reports or other products will come out of the evaluation?
> Who will be responsible for producing the report(s)?
> To whom will the results be presented?
> Who will make the presentations?
> When will results be presented?
> Who will make decisions based on the evaluation results?

Step-by-Step Evaluation Plan

In brief, following the above sequence, a step-by-step evaluation plan can be written. Such a plan identifies what is evaluated, who evaluates, and when and where the evaluation will take place. The plan consists of a timeline, resources, step-by-step procedures for collecting and analyzing information, and plans for reporting the results. An evaluation plan can help one avoid the frustration of having conducted an evaluation that does not provide relevant or valid information.

Informed Decisions　　　One of the fundamental principles of program evaluation is that the evaluation should not be done if it is not going to be used. A well-planned program evaluation can help school personnel and others make informed decisions about how to improve school programs, how to secure resources, and how to help colleagues work together effectively.

Summary

In this introduction, we have presented several reasons for conducting evaluations of school mathematics programs, provided an overview of the contents of this guide, and outlined the general steps or stages for conducting an evaluation. The vignettes in the following section illustrate these points within the context of school mathematics program evaluations.

1 Vignette One

Problem-Solving Instruction

Problem Solving Affects Test Scores

In the 1980s and 1990s, many of the national reports on education pointed to the need to include more problem solving in the mathematics curriculum. This need is especially critical given that technologies like calculators and computers are able to do more and more of the number manipulation and symbol manipulation that has historically been at the center of much of mathematics instruction. High school mathematics courses in particular seem to have heavily emphasized procedural competence over problem solving. Many people feel that scores on standardized tests like the SAT would improve if students were better able to analyze problems and to identify multiple techniques for solving problems.

The faculty at Granger High School have watched the SAT scores of their students decline over the past several years without knowing quite what to do about the decline. Most of the mathematics teachers have now voiced their concerns, so the school is ready to confront the problem of decreasing scores on the mathematics section of the SAT.

Where, What, and Why?

Granger High School is located in the center of downtown Hunterville in Lawrence County. Once a busy, growing city, Hunterville has seen many of its shops close, preferring new locations within malls and shopping centers. Refusing to allow the city to become a ghost town,

10

the local residents fought successfully to restore and revitalize the streets and shopping areas of their town. Downtown Hunterville has now become a pleasant alternative to the fast pace of the local malls.

Granger High School seemed destined to suffer the same fate as many of the city shops. With steady declines in student enrollment, occasional racial tension, inadequate funding, and lack of public interest, Granger High School was in serious trouble. The local school board began to seek justification for closing its doors permanently. Ironically, it was the proposal to close the school that brought about the public interest necessary to save it. Thus, in 1986, Granger began the long road back to rebuilding its reputation as a leading school.

Priorities Need to Be Set

Michelle Rivers became principal of Granger High in 1987. One of her first tasks was to surround herself with hardworking, dedicated faculty and staff members who were open to developing a vision for Granger High School. Ms. Rivers realized that Granger needed improvements in most areas and that all the work could not be done at the same time. Working together with her faculty, a list of priorities was carefully constructed, beginning with the task of making Granger into a school that students wanted to attend, in which faculty members were eager to teach, and where parents wanted to send their teenagers. After 3 years, determination and hard work by both staff and students were making a difference; student enrollment and attendance were increasing, local funding improved dramatically, and community support was growing steadily.

Changing Needs of Students Mean Changes in the School

Granger is one of three county high schools and has 1,200 students in Grades 10 through 12. With 40% black and other minority students, Granger's student body is the most equally balanced racially but it is the most unbalanced economically of the county schools. Many of the students, both white and black, have parents who work in the local manufacturing plants, but many other students have parents who hold executive positions within these companies or who own small businesses. Ms. Rivers and her faculty have worked hard to show students that economics is no barrier to education and that a good education can open doors for everyone. Although less than one third of Granger's students currently go on to college, the number of students interested in college is slowly increasing, and, as a result, more are applying for scholarships and financial aid. SAT scores are an important part of these applications. The faculty of the school, in general, and the faculty of the mathematics department, in particular, are committed to providing the students at Granger with educational opportunities that will make their applications competitive with those of other students.

Because the seven mathematics teachers were concerned about the declines in SAT scores, they asked the senior counselor to do an analysis of the SAT scores over the last decade. His compilation indicated that the average mathematics score had declined 22% over that period, while the verbal score had declined only 17%. The mathematics teachers agreed that the decline of mathematics scores needed to be reversed, so they scheduled a faculty meeting to discuss both the decline and the possible remedies that might help overcome the decline.

Defining the Problem   Two of the teachers felt that students might be deficient in basic mathematics skills and suggested that more drill on basic information in mathematics might be the solution. Greg Hamlin, a second-year teacher, disagreed. He suggested that, because he was closer in time to his own taking of the SAT, he might have a more accurate perspective on the problem. Greg related that, when he took the SAT, and even later the GRE, he found that the most difficult aspect was being flexible in dealing with the content of the items. The test items jumped from one "bit" of content to another, so he had to be quite flexible in trying to call up in his mind the critical concepts and procedures for solving each particular problem. Greg said that, since he began teaching, he noticed a similar difficulty in the way that textbooks tended to teach problem solving. Problem-solving parts of textbooks are isolated from each other; that is, each set of problems typically requires familiarity only with the particular procedure that was dealt with in that lesson. Perhaps, Greg suggested, Granger's students were also having some difficulty dealing with the flexibility required to score well on the SAT because they had rarely had to deal with problems in a single lesson that required more than one solution technique.

Two other teachers said that Greg's comments brought to mind a need for problem solving in the curriculum. One of these teachers said that she had recently been to a conference in which the NCTM's *Curriculum and Evaluation Standards* were discussed, and her perception was that, at least according to the *Standards,* problem solving seemed to be the most critical part of the new recommendations for high school mathematics. Flexibility of thinking reminded her of problem-solving skills. She wondered whether the students at Granger were getting adequate exposure to problem solving, both in quantity and in quality.

Ms. Quantano then suggested that, if students are more successful at solving problems, they are more likely to enjoy mathematics; and, if they like mathematics, they would probably be more interested and willing to take more mathematics courses. Students who take more mathematics courses will usually have a broader mathematics background as well as more experience at problem solving. Such students might be expected to score higher in the mathematics section of the SAT, so they are more likely to get scholarships to college.

Relationship of SAT to Problem Solving

The teachers, then, had conceptualized a chain of thinking that suggested an area of investigation to pursue as a means of understanding the decline in mathematics scores on the SAT. That is, because problem solving seems related to flexibility of thinking, and because flexibility of thinking seems, at least for some people, to be an important part of success on the SAT, then the decline in SAT scores might be explainable if the problem-solving experiences of Granger's students were not adequate either in quantity or quality.

Ms. Bell, the department chair, then asked how much problem solving would be enough and what kinds of problem-solving experiences would demonstrate the high quality they all wanted for the students. Most of the teachers' first reactions were that they did problem solving every day, but, as they began to brainstorm about what would constitute high quality problem-solving experiences, a number of qualities of good problem-solving instruction were listed: interesting to the students, adequate time to think, discussion of different approaches to solutions, illustrative of appropriate mathematics, and providing challenging problems that were appropriate for the ability of the students. Several of the teachers, after considering this list, commented that they might not be exemplifying all of these characteristics in their lessons. Greg suggested that they ought to try to find out which ones of these characteristics they were actually implementing and which they might want to address. The difficulty was in knowing how to go about this assessment.

Ms. Bell remarked that she had recently received two books on evaluation that might be useful in their considerations. One was *Evaluating School Programs: An Educator's Guide* and one was *Mathematics Programs: A Guide to Evaluation*. In particular, she thought that Resource A, on standards and indicators, in *Mathematics Programs* might be a good place to begin consideration of what aspects of problem solving to explore. The teachers agreed to examine *Mathematics Programs* over the next week, so they planned a schedule for circulating the guide. The teachers also asked Ms. Bell to meet with Ms. Rivers to get her reaction to whether their concerns about problem solving were consistent with other plans for improving the instructional program at Granger.

Follow-Up Meeting

Improvements Need to Affect All Students

Ms. Rivers was quite open to discussing how she could support the mathematics faculty in their improvement of problem solving. She agreed with the teachers that an improvement in problem-solving skills among students seemed to have some hope of affecting SAT scores, though she cautioned that improvements might not occur quickly. She also raised the issue that the concern with SAT scores might focus the attention of the mathematics teachers too much on the needs of college-track students and too little on improvements that would benefit all students. She proposed to the teachers that any attempt to improve the problem-solving performance of students should involve all students, not just those in college-track courses. She pointed out that improving the problem-solving performance of all students might also have a payoff in improvements in their scores on the state-mandated competency tests. This would improve the image of Granger High both in the district and throughout the state. She promised them access to some staff development money for workshops on problem solving or for some substitute days for teachers to plan instructional units on problem solving, after they had carried out an evaluation of instruction to determine the most pressing needs for improvement of problem-solving instruction. Further, she supported Ms. Bell's suggestion that the evaluation guides might be a good place to begin looking for assistance.

Most of the teachers were appreciative of the support from Ms. Rivers, but they expressed concern that they probably couldn't deal with the difficulty of improving the problem-solving skills of all students at Granger. After considerable discussion, the teachers agreed that the easiest place to begin their study of problem solving would be with the college-track students, but they also agreed that, once they had made progress toward improving instruction in this area, they would expand their efforts to include all mathematics students in Granger High School. Two teachers expressed concern that some of the students might not ever be capable of learning how to solve problems, but other teachers pointed out that, because teachers were responsible for all students, that it wouldn't be fair to ignore any group.

Focusing the Evaluation

At the next faculty meeting, Ms. Bell asked for suggestions on where to begin the study of problem solving. One of the teachers suggested that Resource A in *Mathematics Programs* had some standards and indicators for problem solving and that those standards might be a useful way to conceptualize what problem solving was all about. The teachers turned to the pages with the standard on problem solving.

1. Mathematics as Problem Solving
    1.1. Students have opportunities to solve problems on a regular basis.
    1.2. Students have opportunities to define problems in both everyday life and mathematical situations.
    1.3. Students have opportunities to develop and carry out plans to solve a wide variety of routine and nonroutine problems, to look back at the original problems to verify and interpret their results, and to generalize solutions and strategies to other situations.

1.4. Students have opportunities to acquire confidence in their ability to use mathematics to solve problems.

Greg said that he thought the two parts of this standard that would have helped him most when he took the SAT were Indicators 1.1 and 1.3; namely, having lots of chances to solve problems and learning how to deal with a wide variety of problems. Ms. Bell asked him what role confidence might have played in his problem-solving performance, and he responded that he thought his confidence would have followed "naturally" from being successful at solving lots of different kinds of problems. He also commented that, although connecting mathematics to the real world was important, his sights had been set so long on going to college that he would have done almost any mathematics problems that his teachers had asked him to do. Two other teachers commented that they thought that real-world applications might be more important for the non-college-bound students—that is, students who probably wouldn't be taking the SAT. They suggested that consideration of Indicator 1.2 therefore might wait until they had dealt with improving problem-solving instruction for students planning to take the SAT. After all, items on the SAT are generally isolated problems and do not deal very much with true, real-world situations.

Possible Sources of Information   Ms. Bell then asked teachers what kind of information they thought was important to evaluation of Indicators 1.1 and 1.3. A variety of suggestions were considered and rejected. The first was counting and classifying the problems in the school's mathematics textbooks. This was rejected because textbooks tend to group similar problems together, so students may not have to think carefully about each problem. These problems might not help students develop the flexibility needed for success on the SAT.

A second suggestion was making a list of sample problems used as examples in instruction. This idea was also rejected, because there was no guarantee that the problems used by teachers as models actually engaged students in problem solving. Students might just be politely watching the teachers work those problems. The teachers did agree, however, that this list would be one way to measure the opportunity for students to see a wide range of problems, so they didn't want to throw out this idea completely. One teacher also raised a concern that writing down all the sample problems might take a lot of teacher time.

The third suggestion was asking students what problems they have solved. This was quickly dismissed, because it was agreed that students might not be able to distinguish clearly between problems and exercises. That is, students might classify anything they were asked to do as a problem.

A fourth suggestion was to observe classes to see what problems were used by teachers and what problems were solved by students. There was an extended silence after this suggestion, until one of the teachers said she might be intimidated by having other teachers come in to observe her. This scheme seemed to be too much like the state's required teacher evaluation procedure. Two other teachers quickly agreed with this concern, so they moved on to another idea.

Good Ideas Must Be Developed

The fifth suggestion was examining lesson plans to see how problems were included in the planning of instruction. Although this idea was related to the notion of teacher observation, everyone agreed that it would be less threatening. After all, they could remove their names from the lesson plans so that their identities might be at least partially hidden. Greg suggested that they might also want to examine students' work to see how the problem solving modeled by teachers was actually being used by students. Ms. Bell responded quite enthusiastically to this idea and commented that, because the goal was to improve students' performance, at least part of the evaluation of their program ought to focus on student outcomes. Discussion quickly focused on the notions that these sources of data would fit Indicator 1.3 nicely and Indicator 1.1 somewhat less well. That is, examination of teachers' lesson plans would reveal information about the extent of opportunity students had to engage in problem solving, but it would also reveal the ways that problem solving was modeled for students. If teachers don't demonstrate how to decide on what plans to use, how to carry out those plans, how to interpret the results, and how to generalize to other problems, then students are not likely to develop these skills. Examination of student work would reveal how well the students were internalizing what they had an opportunity to learn, that is, how well the students were able to address each of the major parts of the problem-solving process. It is only internalized knowledge that students are likely to use in situations like taking the SAT. Thus, by the end of this conversation, the teachers had decided that Indicator 1.3 would be the main focus of their evaluation.

The Evaluation Instrument

Evaluation of Lesson Plans and Student Work

The next task was to agree on ways to carry out the evaluations of lesson plans and students' work. A checklist seemed the most obvious way to make the evaluation as objective as possible. A checklist would allow teachers to compare each lesson plan or piece of student work against an agreed-upon standard; the checklists could then be summarized by a subgroup of the teachers. The difficulty was in deciding on the categories to include in the checklist.

Everyone agreed that one category was a measure of the amount of problem solving planned for a lesson. Suggestions on how to make this measurement included counting the number of examples planned for discussion and estimating the percentage of class time that might be spent in discussing problems with students. Ms. Quantano said she didn't like either technique. A count of problems might encourage teachers to address a large number of problems in a class period; but this could actually work against any in-depth treatment of particular problems. Counting alone might encourage superficial instruction on problems. On the other hand, trying to estimate the percentage of time spent on problems would be difficult and would probably not yield reliable data. Ms. Bell then suggested that examining a series of lesson plans for each teacher might reveal the consistency of attention given to problem solving in instruction. Consensus was easily reached on this compromise position.

A somewhat more difficult task was how to measure the quality of experiences of problem solving. Greg said that he often thought about what problem-solving strategies he should teach, so it might be useful to list some of the more common strategies. He offered several as a start on such a list: make a table, draw a picture, write an equation, and model with manipulatives. Ms. Quantano again said that she thought the discussion was getting sidetracked. Identifying a strategy is only one part of the problem-solving process; prior to identifying a strategy, students need to analyze the problem to see what they know and what they are to find out, and, after identifying a strategy, students need to carry out the strategy and then reflect on whether its application resulted in an answer that made sense. Greg conceded that he had overlooked a lot of these concerns. Two teachers thought that Ms. Quantano's outline of the problem-solving strategy might be turned into a set of criteria not only for evaluating students' work but also for characterizing teachers' modeling of problem solving in a lesson plan.

Ms. Bell then led a discussion of what those categories might be. The first suggestion was analyze, strategize, act, reflect, generalize. Three teachers expressed discomfort, because the list seemed to place so little emphasis on skills that students were expected to carry out on paper. How can you tell if a student analyzes? Or strategizes? Or reflects? These teachers thought that more emphasis needed to be placed on things that students could demonstrate on paper. Greg argued, however, that the real key to problem solving, as opposed to merely copying what a teacher modeled, was skill in analyzing a problem and choosing a strategy that would generate the solution. He further speculated that good problem solvers probably are also good at reflecting and generalizing, but these skills are not likely to be observed on a single problem; rather, they would be noticed as a pattern of performance across lots of problem-solving experiences. Ms. Quantano supported his position but also expressed concern about how to actually measure these important skills either in students' work or in lesson plans. The teachers agreed that more time was needed to develop the categories to include on the checklist, so they adjourned until the next faculty meeting.

Considerations in Developing a Checklist

Two weeks later, the teachers returned to the problem of setting up categories. Ms. Quantano began the discussion by saying that she had begun to examine both her lesson plans and her students' work in light of the discussion on problem solving. She felt it was reasonable for her to indicate in her lesson plans when and how she would ask questions that highlighted analysis of a problem and the ways that she chose potential strategies to use to solve a problem. She had had some difficulty, however, trying to structure student assignments so that the assignments could give her the same information about the students' thinking. She had decided that to do so would significantly alter the ways that she handled problem solving in her classes. Should she begin to make such alterations now, or should those changes wait until the evaluation was completed? After a few minutes of discussion, the group decided that she should wait. The goal of this evaluation was to gather information about the current state of instruction on problem solving. If the evaluation revealed weaknesses, then changes could be planned to address those weaknesses specifically.

Mr. Johnston noted that one type of category that had been omitted from the earlier discussion was the notion of translating information into the symbolism of mathematics. Three other teachers immediately agreed that translation was an important part of mathematics problem solving and should not be omitted. They also agreed that translation was so important that it probably ought to be separated from the symbol manipulation that students were expected to do once the symbols were written. Ms. Quantano suggested that the categories of analysis and strategy selection might be combined, because it probably would be difficult to specify clearly how they were to be measured. Ms. Bell suggested that, similarly, the categories of reflection and generalization might also need to be combined; again, it might be very difficult to find ways to clearly distinguish between them.

Discussion went on for about another half hour, but finally consensus was reached on a set of four categories that needed to be included in the checklist:

Checklist Categories

- *Analysis:* identification of the knowns and unknowns in a problem, identifying potential strategies, selecting one strategy to use
- *Translation:* finding mathematical symbols to represent the information
- *Action:* performing symbolic manipulations and calculations
- *Verification:* checking the answer, deciding reasonableness of the answer, generalizing to other situations

Two checklists needed to be created, one for evaluation of lesson plans and one for evaluation of students' work. The teachers decided to let Ms. Bell, Mr. Johnston, and Ms. Quantano work on formatting the two versions.

Collecting Data   The teachers then turned their attention to the problems surrounding the gathering of data. They first brainstormed the questions that they thought needed to be answered. How much data should they gather? When should they gather data? How could the data be organized and summarized? Who would have access to the data?

The first questions they addressed were related to how much data were to be gathered and when those data were to be gathered. Two kinds of data were to be collected: lesson plans and students' work. Because it was already about the middle of the school year, the teachers realized that they could either go back to previously developed lesson plans or they could plan to gather lesson plans from future lessons. Ms. Bell asked what differences might be observed if lesson plans from a previous month were compared with lesson plans developed a week or two from this meeting. Ms. Quantano suggested that, if she had time to plan a lesson around the ideas of problem solving, she might set aside more class time to work on problems and she might make more explicit notations in her lesson plans about how to focus students' attention on various aspects of the problem-solving process. Previous lessons might reflect more attention to content, without as much explicit attention to problem solving. Two other teachers said that they thought that content was still the most important outcome of their instruction; they said they didn't think that there would be very much difference in the way they organized their lesson plans, especially in light of the fact that the state had mandated that lesson plans had to include (but were not necessarily restricted to) particular elements: state objectives; provide instruction on the new materials; check to see if students have grasped the material; provide directed practice; summarize the day's work. Mr. Johnston said that, even if there might not be any differences in the lesson plans, it might be worthwhile to evaluate previous lessons and future lessons, just to be sure that there were no differences.

Outside Resources   Ms. Bell asked if any of the teachers would have any objections to comparing lesson plans from several different times. There was a noticeable silence before three of the teachers almost simultaneously said that they would not mind. The rest of the teachers voiced agreement, so Ms. Bell said that they needed to be careful to get enough information about each teacher so that the data would support reliable conclusions. She suggested that they review the section of the *Educator's Guide* that deals with guidelines on reliability of measurements.

They found that this section gave some good help in understanding the nature of reliability, but it did not give explicit information on sample size requirements, so they turned to other resource material for help. After considering this information, Greg suggested that it might be best to look at about four lesson plans for each teacher: one from about 6 weeks ago, one from about 2 weeks ago, one from the current week, and one from 3 weeks from this time. This much data would allow patterns to be observed across the time when the teachers started to think collectively about the role of problem solving in instruction. Because the teachers had earlier agreed to restrict their attention to college-track students, the teachers considered whether to use lessons from Geometry, Algebra II, or Pre-Calculus. At this point in the school year, most of the time in Geometry courses was being spent on writing proofs, so the teachers felt that they were using a greater variety of instructional techniques in Algebra II and Pre-Calculus. Each teacher was teaching at least one of those classes, so they agreed to gather the lessons from those courses. The teachers agreed that analyzing four lesson plans ought to give some interesting information about the ways that they incorporated problem solving in their lessons.

Discussion then turned to determining how much student work needed to be examined. Ms. Quantano suggested that they try to gather some student work from the last two lessons for which the lesson plans were being evaluated. Because student work had not been saved from the earlier part of the year, all student data would have to be gathered from current and future lessons. This meant gathering student work from a lesson this week and from a lesson 3 weeks from this time. Ms. Bell suggested that two or three student papers from each lesson might be enough to examine. Again, the teachers turned to the section of the *Educator's Guide* that dealt with reliability of data. After considering the guidelines, they agreed that three sample papers from each lesson would provide a reasonable amount of data. They further agreed that each teacher should select one paper from the best two or three students, one paper from the middle section of the class, and one paper from the three or four students at the bottom of the class. This would provide a cross section of information from each classroom. Because it had already been agreed that eventually all students needed to improve in problem-solving performance, information from a variety of students might be useful for developing an improvement plan for the school.

Summarizing Data   The teachers agreed that the problem of summarizing data would probably be addressed following completion of the coding sheets that were being developed by Ms. Bell, Mr. Johnston, and Ms. Quantano. Because the data were to be collected from Algebra II and Pre-Calculus classes, it would be important that the summary provide information that would help in understanding the role of problem solving for that content.

Ms. Bell then raised concerns about how the information should be reported back to teachers and about who would have access to the lesson plans and the student work. She felt that it was important to avoid any possibility for comparisons to be made of individuals, because the problem was a departmental problem rather than a problem of specific individuals. Mr. Johnston suggested that, if the teachers removed all names from the documents, the documents could be evaluated on the basis of their substance, quite apart from the personality of the individual who prepared the document. There was no objection to this plan, but the teachers agreed that Ms. Bell should choose a letter to write on the lesson plans and student papers for each teacher so that the data for each of the teachers could be compared. Ms. Quantano suggested that all of the lesson plans and student work should be available for all the teachers to study, but two other teachers said they were uncomfortable with this plan, saying that to do so would create the expectation that all teachers ought to spend the time to look at all the documents. Ms. Bell suggested that the purpose of gathering data as part of the solution to a problem is to find patterns in the data that might suggest some solution to the problem. Pattern finding rests on looking at the global characteristics of data, not the individual bits of data. Individual bits of information sometimes represent unusual or extreme cases that might not actually be important in formulating the solution to a problem. She argued therefore that they might better invest their time in examining the summaries of the data to look for patterns rather than in examining all of the cases. Ms. Quantano was convinced by this argument, agreeing that only the summaries of the data needed to be distributed to the teachers.

Developing the Checklist

Ms. Bell, Mr. Johnston, and Ms. Quantano met the next day to plan the checklist that would be used. They reviewed the categories that the teachers had suggested:

- *Analysis:* identification of the knowns and unknowns, identifying potential strategies, selecting one strategy to use
- *Translation:* finding mathematical symbols to represent the information
- *Action:* performing symbolic manipulations and calculations
- *Verification:* checking the answer, deciding reasonableness of the answer, generalizing to other situations

---

Problem-Solving Lesson Plan Review Sheet

| | The lesson shows evidence of teaching students about | | | |
| Teacher | Analysis | Translation | Action | Verification |

Problem-Solving Student Work Review Sheet

| | The student work shows evidence of | | | |
| Student | Analysis | Translation | Action | Verification |

Figure 1.1. Checklists

As they talked, they realized that they could apply the same categories to both kinds of data, so they decided that only one checklist needed to be created. It seemed to them that all they had to do was identify whether a lesson plan or a student's paper reflected effort in each of these categories. The most difficult part of the data gathering would be to get the teachers to agree on when there was adequate evidence for effort in a particular category. Their final checklist is presented in Figure 1.1.

Thinking About Reliability

To help the teachers understand the checklists, Ms. Bell suggested that the teachers might want to practice with a sample of student work. She offered to get some samples from her class. (See Figure 1.2.) At the next faculty meeting, she distributed copies of the sample student work and asked the teachers individually to identify whether the work exemplified each of the categories. After each teacher made an individual decision, Ms. Bell asked them to work in pairs and discuss their decisions. Once those discussions were concluded, Ms. Bell led a group discussion of their evaluations.

Ms. Quantano started the discussion of the first sample by commenting that she had rarely seen such complete work. The picture shows a very thorough analysis of the problem; the original patio is drawn inside the expanded patio, and all dimensions are labeled. Translation is evident in the first equation written; the relationship expressed is accurate for the expanded patio. The action in manipulating the symbols to reach a solution is accurate and includes every step. The crossing off of the answer, −16, indicates that the student realized that a length in the real world could not be negative. Verification is evident from the fact that the dimensions of the enlarged patio are written down and then multiplied to get the correct area of 165 square feet. The only minor deficiency is that the student did not

---

Problem:

> Gertrude's house has a square patio, but it is too small. She wants to en-
> large it so that the area will be 165 square feet. She can expand the patio
> by 5 feet in one direction and by 1 foot in the other. What are the dimen-
> sions of the new patio?

Student 1

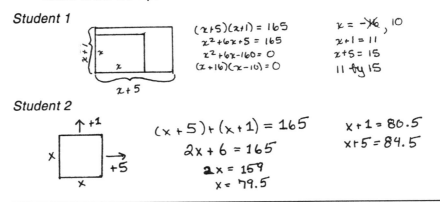

$$(x+5)(x+1) = 165$$
$$x^2 + 6x + 5 = 165$$
$$x^2 + 6x - 160 = 0$$
$$(x+16)(x-10) = 0$$

$$x = -16, \ 10$$
$$x + 1 = 11$$
$$x + 5 = 15$$
$$11 \ \text{by} \ 15$$

Student 2

$$(x+5) + (x+1) = 165$$
$$2x + 6 = 165$$
$$2x = 159$$
$$x = 79.5$$

$$x + 1 = 80.5$$
$$x + 5 = 84.5$$

Figure 1.2. Sample Student Work

write in the units of length (i.e., feet) in the final answer. All of the
other teachers agreed that this was a very easy problem to match to
the categories on the checklist.

The second sample, however, provided more of a challenge for the
teachers. Mr. Johnston started the discussion by commenting that the
diagram was basically correct, though it was not as clearly drawn as
it might have been. He said that he would give credit for analysis. The
translation, however, was not accurate. Instead of writing the product
of the new dimensions, the student wrote the sum. This might indicate some confusion between the ideas of area and perimeter. This
student, then, should not get credit for translation. The manipulation
of symbols (i.e., action) was correct *in the context of the wrong translation.* The student added 1 and 5 to the solution to get dimensions
of a new patio, but there was no verification that the solution was
actually correct. If the student had even estimated 80.5 times 84.5 as
being greater than 80 times 80 (which is 6,400), the incorrectness of
this "solution" would have been evident. This student would seem to
get credit for analysis and action but not for translation and verification. One of the other teachers questioned whether the student really
had adequately analyzed the problem; the arrows with "+1" and "+5"
might simply be from the student's writing down some of the information in the problem. Maybe the student didn't really understand that
the dimensions were increasing. During the ensuing discussion, Ms.
Bell commented that so many students didn't even draw a picture
that she felt this student really had demonstrated analysis, even if it
wasn't a complete analysis. Her argument swayed the group, and they
agreed that the student should get credit for analysis.

Analysis of Results

Coding the Data   Photocopies of the lesson plans from the lessons already completed and from this week's lesson along with student work from this week's lesson were gathered by the teachers, with names having been removed prior to the papers being given to Ms. Bell. Ms. Bell wrote different letters and numbers on the lesson plans so that each teacher's lesson plans could be matched and so that the time the lesson was taught could be identified. Part of each of the next two departmental meetings was devoted to coding these data according to the instruments presented earlier. At the outset, the teachers agreed that they would of course not code their own lessons or the work of their own students. They agreed that, if they picked up a paper they recognized, they would simply exchange it for another. By the time plans for the fourth lesson, along with accompanying student work, were turned in, more than half of the earlier data were coded. Several teachers were surprised at the amount of work required to complete the coding of the data, but they persevered for another 3 weeks until all of the data were completely coded.

Early in the process, Ms. Bell asked the teachers to work in pairs on the coding to be sure that they were looking for the same attributes in both the lesson plans and the student work. Although there were no formal intercoder reliability studies conducted for these data, the discussions in faculty meetings during the coding sessions provided a rich interchange about the nature of problem solving and the ways that one could recognize when problem solving was taking place. Several times, the teachers commented that the practice session with the sample student work was important in helping them make their decisions about whether there was evidence for each category. The final data are presented in Tables 1.1 and 1.2.

Interpretation

In Table 1.1, the letters indicate the teachers and the numbers indicate the sequence when the lessons were taught. Several different patterns emerge from these data. First, all of the teachers addressed the action part of problem solving in each lesson. This is not surprising, given the fact that manipulation skills are so heavily emphasized in textbooks. Further help for teachers on how to teach manipulation skills would seem unnecessary.

Second, the teachers seemed to react somewhat differently to the task of teaching problem solving. Teachers A, B, and E seem to have made an effort to include more parts of problem solving in their instruction, while teachers C and D do not seem to have changed their instruction as much as time passed. Teacher E seems to have tried to

TABLE 1.1   Problem-Solving Lesson Plan Review Sheet

| | *The lesson shows evidence of teaching students about* | | | |
Teacher	Analysis	Translation	Action	Verification
A-1	no	yes	yes	no
A-2	no	no	yes	no
A-3	no	yes	yes	yes
A-4	yes	yes	yes	yes
B-1	no	no	yes	yes
B-2	no	no	yes	yes
B-3	yes	no	yes	no
B-4	yes	yes	yes	no
C-1	yes	yes	yes	no
C-2	yes	yes	yes	no
C-3	yes	yes	yes	no
C-4	yes	yes	yes	yes
D-1	no	yes	yes	yes
D-2	no	no	yes	yes
D-3	no	yes	yes	yes
D-4	no	yes	yes	yes
E-1	no	no	yes	no
E-2	no	no	yes	no
E-3	no	no	yes	yes
E-4	no	yes	yes	no

incorporate two new elements in instruction but wasn't successful in getting both new elements in at the same time. Teacher C seems to regularly incorporate most of the elements of problem solving in instruction. At least some of the teachers might profit from inservice training on ways to coordinate all the elements of problem solving in instruction.

Identifying New Problem Areas

Third, each teacher was able to incorporate translation and verification in at least one lesson but some teachers were not able to include analysis in any of their lessons. It appears that most of the teachers might profit from some inservice training on ways to analyze problems and then on ways to incorporate analysis into instruction.

In Table 1.2, the uppercase letters indicate the teachers; the numbers indicate whether the student paper was from the lowest range (1) or the middle range (2) or the upper range (3) of students; and the lowercase letters indicate whether the paper was associated with the third (a) or the fourth (b) lesson being analyzed. Several different patterns emerge from these data. First, most of the students were able

TABLE 1.2 Problem-Solving Student Work Review Sheet

Student	Analysis	The student work shows evidence of Translation	Action	Verification
A-1a	no	yes	yes	no
A-1b	no	no	no	no
A-2a	no	yes	yes	no
A-2b	no	yes	yes	yes
A-3a	no	yes	yes	no
A-3b	no	yes	yes	yes
B-1a	no	no	yes	no
B-1b	no	no	yes	no
B-2a	yes	no	no	no
B-2b	no	no	no	no
B-3a	no	yes	yes	no
B-3b	yes	yes	yes	no
C-1a	no	yes	yes	no
C-1b	no	yes	yes	no
C-2a	yes	no	yes	no
C-2b	yes	yes	yes	no
C-3a	yes	yes	yes	no
C-3b	yes	yes	yes	yes
D-1a	no	no	yes	no
D-1b	no	yes	yes	no
D-2a	no	yes	yes	no
D-2b	no	yes	yes	yes
D-3a	no	no	yes	yes
D-3b	no	yes	yes	yes
E-1a	no	no	yes	no
E-1b	no	no	yes	no
E-2a	no	no	yes	yes
E-2b	no	no	yes	yes
E-3a	no	yes	yes	no
E-3b	no	yes	yes	yes

to show how they carried out the manipulation of the symbols for problem solving. This is not surprising, given the attention that the teachers gave to this part of problem solving.

Second, students in the upper range of the classes generally demonstrated more of the elements of problem solving. This also is not surprising. In fact, it suggests that teachers were fairly accurate in assessing the levels of performance of their students.

Third, students demonstrated analysis least often in their work. Again, this is not surprising, given that the teachers seem to have omitted this element most often from instruction. In general, the performance of the students appears to match fairly closely the way that instruction was organized. When a teacher successfully included one of the elements of problem solving in instruction, the students appear to be much more likely to be able to demonstrate that element in their work. This is certainly an encouraging trend!

Use of Results

Based on the analysis of the data, the teachers decided to make a formal presentation to Ms. Rivers and then ask her to provide some funds for a series of inservice sessions on the teaching of problem solving. In particular, the teachers felt they needed the most help in learning how to teach students to analyze problems clearly and in learning how to coordinate all aspects of problem solving in instruction. The teachers recognized that improvements in SAT scores was not going to be observed for some time. The first step was to improve the delivery of problem-solving instruction to students.

The development of a "template" for students to use as they completed problem solving was one idea that Ms. Bell had for a first step. She imagined a page divided into four sections with one of the four headings in each section. There might be one or two generic questions under each heading to focus the students' attention on the essential features of that heading. For example, for the analysis section, the questions might be as follows: "What do you know?" "What do you need to find out?" "Can you draw a picture to represent the problem?" Forcing students to address these questions might keep their attention focused on the main elements of the problem.

Ms. Rivers was impressed with the evaluation the teachers conducted and was pleased to provide funds for the inservice sessions. She suggested that Ms. Bell write a brief evaluation report to keep on file in both the mathematics department office and her office.

Summary of Evaluation Principles

This example illustrates several important principles that should be kept in mind during all evaluations of school programs.

1. Do not attempt to evaluate every aspect of a program at once. Focus the evaluation by selecting one or two important aspects of a few standards and indicators of quality. The faculty were faced with a difficult problem: how to increase SAT scores. Problem solving was only one important component of the solution, but it was an excellent choice for beginning. Learning how to teach problem solving

effectively takes considerable time. Teachers shouldn't expect to be wildly successful the first few times they try it.

2. When choosing a method for data collection, select an alternative that minimizes the burden on those who are asked to provide information. The teachers were rightfully concerned about the amount of their time that would be required in gathering information. Information gathering is critical for evaluation, but the expectation that teachers will gather the data must be balanced by the realization that data gathering will have to be an "add on" to regular instructional duties. If too much time were asked for, teachers might not be able to give it, and the data might not be gathered.

3. Ask questions that can be answered directly, and avoid questions that require speculation. The data gathered in this example were generated from information that was readily available. Because the teachers were involved as a group in analyzing the lesson plans and the student work, they had a greater understanding of and appreciation for the interpretation of the results. A quite different view, and possibly not as accurate a view, of how problem solving was being taught and learned would have been generated by asking teachers for their general impressions of how much time they spent on problem solving. It is often difficult for teachers to separate their sense of how much time they spend on a topic from the importance they give to that topic.

4. Collect information that will not only help identify areas of program strength and weakness but also guide remedial action when improvement is needed. The categories used to analyze problem-solving instruction and student work in the checklist were selected by the teachers as those most important for the overall process of problem solving. The data clearly show that the teachers and their students need help in understanding the analysis aspect of problem solving. It was appropriate for the teachers to suggest that they would profit from some inservice workshop sessions on analyzing problems.

5. Whenever possible, seek information from more than one source. The use of information from teachers and samples of students' work generated a more accurate picture than either one of those sources of information would have by itself. Additional information from an outside observer, both of what teachers were actually focusing on in instruction and of ways that students approached problem solving, might be valuable during a second round of evaluation.

Alternatives to the Strategy Used Here

Other Sources and Ways of Collecting Information

Because Standard 1, "Mathematics as Problem Solving," deals primarily with behaviors and actions that take place within classrooms, the evaluation team felt that the information could best be obtained through data obtained from classrooms. Classroom observations would probably have yielded a different kind of information, but, because of the threat that this technique posed to the teachers, it was rejected. A student questionnaire concerning the frequency and type of problem solving taking place in their classes would have yielded an even different view. As was pointed out by the teachers, however, students may not be aware of the true meaning of problem solving and some may think that all of mathematics consists of a series of problems to solve. As the teachers become more comfortable with teaching problem solving, they will likely want to consider other ways of assessing the quality of their instruction.

Cautions Regarding Misinterpretation

Because the checklist data show that none of the teachers taught every aspect of problem solving in every lesson, it would be easy to assume that no one is teaching problem solving in the classroom. This certainly was not the case. All of the teachers were teaching problem solving at some level. It is important to identify particular areas of difficulty and to plan actions that will help overcome those difficulties.

Evaluations May Raise More Questions

Also, because the mathematics teachers were already giving some attention to problem solving, it would be easy to suggest that giving more attention to problem solving would not improve SAT scores. The mathematics teachers at Granger may, in fact, have expected to find greater deficiencies in problem-solving opportunities for students. It is important to remember that underlying causes for complex problems are not always obvious and that the purpose of a self-study is to begin to understand the depth of those problems rather than to seek easy solutions. Keep in mind, as well, that effective problem solving requires *all* of the elements listed in the checklist. Sometimes an evaluation must find alternative reasons for a persistent problem. Therefore it is not surprising that the faculty would want some help in learning how to teach problem solving and would want to continue to examine the possible factors that might contribute to the decreasing SAT scores at Granger.

2

Vignette Two

Student Placement: Evaluating the Transition From Arithmetic to Algebra

The *Curriculum and Evaluation Standards for School Mathematics* (National Council of Teachers of Mathematics, 1989) calls for an algebra strand even in middle school. After reading this report, Mr. Burton, principal of Lincoln Middle School, recalled some conversations he had had with the mathematics teachers in his building about the increasing number of students from Lincoln Middle School who were failing Algebra I after they moved on to high school. The teachers were concerned about whether their students were being adequately prepared for algebra, and, if not, how the teachers could better prepare the students.

Where, What, and Why?

Lincoln Middle School is located within the city limits of the town of Burnsville. Lincoln was built in the late 1960s and enrolls 450 students in Grades 6 through 8. Burnsville, a city of 18,000, is supported by a variety of manufacturing industries, ranging from household appliances to mobile homes. Students come to Lincoln from two elementary schools, also located within the city. On average, students at Lincoln are from predominately low- or middle-income families; 65% of the students are black and 35% are white.

Jim Burton became principal of Lincoln 8 years ago. During that time, Lincoln has maintained steady enrollment figures and almost no turnover in faculty and staff. Mr. Burton, one of two black principals in the county, is proud of his staff of 20 teachers (4 of whom are mathematics teachers), 1 school counselor, 1 media specialist, and 2 secretaries. He maintains a well-organized school and has gained the respect and cooperation of all his staff members. Mr. Burton is well liked by the students at Lincoln and is well respected within the school community. Parents, students, and teachers alike view him as an educational leader who is supportive and fair minded.

Articulation Between Courses

During the past 3 or 4 years, mathematics teachers at Lincoln have repeatedly expressed growing concern over the students who were enrolled in ninth-grade Algebra I classes. When percentages of failures for these students were compared with those from previous years, the failure rate seemed to be increasing. Mr. Hughes, lead teacher for the mathematics department, in consultation with Mr. Burton, decided to raise the concern about the increasing failure rate at a departmental meeting to see what might be done to remedy the situation. Mr. Burton passed on to Mr. Hughes *Evaluating School Programs: An Educator's Guide*, which had recently been distributed at a meeting of all principals in the district. Mr. Hughes volunteered to check with the district's curriculum coordinator to see if she had a copy of the *Mathematics Programs: A Guide to Evaluation* that was referenced in the *Educator's Guide*. The curriculum coordinator pointed out that the standards and indicators (Resource A) in the *Mathematics Programs: A Guide to Evaluation* might prove to be very useful to the department faculty as they considered what to do about the Algebra I failure rate.

Program Evaluation Should Not Be a Threat to Teachers

It seemed obvious from the outset of the meeting that the faculty who taught the eighth-grade mathematics course felt they were being blamed for the recent failures. Mr. Burton and Mr. Hughes were quick to reassure everyone present that no one was at fault, and in fact the main purpose for the meeting was to discuss the problem to find out first if there was a problem and, if so, how they might begin to tackle it.

Focusing the Evaluation

Sometimes it is difficult to pinpoint which factors in a child's educational experiences bring success and which bring frustration and failure. Therefore the teachers at Lincoln realized the evaluation process before them was no simple task. Time and money were both in short supply, so the teachers realized that they couldn't expect a lot of help from outside consultants. The teachers were, however, very interested in the welfare of their students and realized that having so many students fail algebra didn't help either the students or the teachers' reputations.

The first approach Mr. Hughes used was to ask faculty (Ms. Chinn, Mrs. Lasha, Ms. Townsend, and himself) to brainstorm about what they thought might be the causes of a student's failing Algebra I. The suggestions were wide ranging:

1. Students might not be working hard enough in Algebra I.
2. Students were not adequately prepared for Algebra I.
3. Students were misplaced by high school counselors in Algebra I when they needed to take Pre-Algebra.
4. High school teachers don't care enough about students to help those in trouble.
5. High school students have too many outside activities.
6. Too many high school students are working part-time so they don't have time to study.

Standards and Indicators Reflect Changes in Mathematics Curriculum

When the suggestion about inadequate preparation was made, Mrs. Lasha asked if the content of Algebra I was the same as it was when she taught it 8 years ago. Mr. Hughes had taken the suggestion of the curriculum coordinator and had brought his copy of the *Mathematics Programs: A Guide to Evaluation* to the meeting so that the faculty could examine the standards for algebra. He opened *Mathematics Programs* to Resource A, which contained the standards and indicators, and began a short discussion of the changing nature of mathematics. Of course, these standards and indicators are consistent with the vision of mathematics as outlined in the *Curriculum and Evaluation Standards* (NCTM, 1989), so he was easily able to relate the two documents. He also pointed out that, because they were talking about students who were getting ready for algebra, it might be useful to consider the standards for content that were important as a foundation for algebra; namely, Standard 5, "Number, Numeration, and Computation," and Standard 6, "Patterns and Functions," as well as Standard 10, "Algebra" (see Resource A).

Ms. Townsend asked if they might postpone further discussion of the original problem of algebra failures so that they would each have a chance to study the standards in *Mathematics Programs*. Mr. Hughes agreed that this was an excellent idea, but he asked the teachers to think about the new standards in light of the ways that they were teaching mathematics currently. Perhaps by trying to apply the standards to their own teaching, they might have a better sense of how the standards might also be applied to the teaching of algebra. (The three standards being focused on are presented below.) The faculty agreed to meet the following week.

5. Number, Numeration, and Computation
    5.1. Students have opportunities to develop increasingly sophisticated concepts about numbers (i.e., whole numbers, integers, common and decimal fractions, irrational and complex numbers) and to understand and appreciate the need for numbers beyond the whole numbers.
    5.2. Students have opportunities to construct number meanings through real-world experience and the use of physical materials, to understand counting, grouping, and place-value concepts, to develop and use order relations for numbers, and to interpret the multiple uses of numbers in the real world.
    5.3. Students have opportunities to explore estimation strategies, including recognizing when estimation is appropriate or inappropriate, determining reasonableness of results, and applying estimation in working with quantities, measurement, computation, and problem solving.
    5.4. Students have opportunities to understand how the basic arithmetic operations are related to one another.
    5.5. Students have opportunities to acquire reasonable proficiency with basic facts and algorithms, including those for whole numbers, fractions, decimals, integers, and rational numbers and to use a variety of mental computation and estimation techniques.
    5.6. Students have opportunities to learn how to select and use computational techniques appropriate to specific problems, including the use of calculators of various types.

6. Patterns and Functions
    6.1. Students have opportunities to recognize, describe, extend, and create a wide variety of patterns and to use patterns to analyze mathematical situations.
    6.2. Students have opportunities to explore the use of variables, open sentences, tables, graphs, verbal rules, and equations to describe and express relationships.
    6.3. Students have opportunities to analyze functional relationships to explain how a change in one quantity results in a change in another.
    6.4. Students have opportunities to model real-world phenomena with a variety of functions.
    6.5. Students have opportunities to recognize that a variety of problem situations can be modeled by the same type of function.

10. Algebra
    10.1. Students have opportunities to understand the concepts of variable, expression, and equation.

10.2. Students have opportunities to represent situations and number patterns with tables, graphs, verbal rules, expressions, equations and inequalities and explore the interrelationships of these representations.

10.3. Students have opportunities to develop confidence in solving linear equations using concrete, informal, and formal methods.

10.4. Students have opportunities to apply algebraic methods to solve a variety of real-world and mathematical problems.

10.5. Students have opportunities to study mathematical structures.

10.6. Students have opportunities to study trigonometry and the conceptual underpinnings of calculus.

At the follow-up meeting, Ms. Chinn began the discussion by commenting that the new standards didn't seem to address the need for students to be able to compute. "Where does it say that students will learn how to do paper-and-pencil work like they will have to do on the standardized tests we give every spring?" Mrs. Lasha replied that, given the availability of calculators, it didn't seem as important for students to master paper-and-pencil skills as it might have a decade or so ago. Mr. Hughes raised the question of whether it might be true that a focus on computation might be inconsistent with the instructional focus of the high school. Ms. Townsend agreed that it might, but she wondered if the high school was really doing what the new standards indicated were important to do.

Mismatch Between Middle School and High School Curriculum

Mr. Hughes said that a similar thought had crossed his mind during the week, so he had called the chair of the mathematics department in the high school to get a feel for their Algebra I curriculum. The high school mathematics department chair told him that the Algebra I curriculum had been rewritten about 3 years ago by the state's department of education to be more in line with standards like those in *Mathematics Programs*. The state department consultant had even mentioned in a talk at a recent meeting of high school mathematics department chairpersons that he thought the recently published standards in *Mathematics Programs* were a good model of standards that were consistent with the thrust of the revised curriculum. Mr. Hughes said that, at this point in the conversation, he was thinking that there might be some degree of mismatch between the focus of Lincoln's instruction and the expectations of the high school Algebra I teachers, so he extended the conversation by asking about the way that students were placed in Algebra I in ninth grade. The high school used three types of information: end-of-year tests from the eighth-grade, grades in eighth-grade mathematics courses, and individual teacher recommendations that the eighth-grade teachers complete every year for every student. The high school teachers feel that, because the eighth-grade teachers know the students very well, the individual recommendations are given the heaviest weight among the three types of information. He said that perhaps Indicator 17.6 might be the best one to guide their thinking:

> 17.6. Counselors and mathematics teachers maintain effective communication for advising students about program decisions and for planning of instructional schedules.

"Perhaps we need better communication among teachers in our buildings so that students can be appropriately placed in advanced courses."

Ms. Chinn said that, because she was very concerned about the computational skills of her students, she had always centered her evaluations of students on mastery of those computation skills. She said that in particular she had never thought about the need for students to have the confidence to do algebra or for understanding interrelationships among representations of ideas. Mrs. Lasha said that, because students were often so unsure of themselves, just because of all the changes associated with being adolescents, she felt she had to encourage those students who really put effort into class by completing their homework and other assignments. She said that students who tried hard were the ones that she tended to recommend for more mathematics courses. Ms. Townsend and Mr. Hughes said that they tended to take into account the standardized tests in making individual recommendations, but they both realized during the past week that the test was more oriented toward basic computational skills rather than conceptual understanding or problem solving. Consequently, they also felt that they might be recommending the wrong kind of student for algebra.

Correlating Placement Information With Success in Algebra I

Mr. Hughes then asked what they might consider doing to test out their concern about whether the recommendations for individual students were effective mechanisms to use in placing students in Algebra I. Ms. Chinn said that she was currently enrolled in a research course as part of her master's degree program in mathematics education, and they were currently studying the use of correlations to investigate relationships among variables. Was it possible, she asked, to find out which of the three types of information—test scores, grades, or teacher recommendations—were effective predictors for success in Algebra I? She would ask her professor and report back at the faculty meeting the following week.

At the next meeting, Ms. Chinn did report that correlations seemed to be one way to begin to investigate whether the placement process was adequate. Her professor had agreed to let her gather the appropriate data, analyze it, and use the analysis as her project for the course she was taking.

Gathering and Analyzing the Data

Thinking About a Sample

At the next meeting of the faculty, there was an intense discussion of the data that seemed most appropriate to gather. The faculty agreed that they should gather several pieces of data for each student: eighth-grade course grade, standardized test score, teacher recommendation, and grade in Algebra I. Their discussion then turned to how much data would be gathered. Ms. Chinn suggested that they should go back 5 years, because the new curriculum was only 3 years old. They could then compute correlations for three subsets of the data: the 2 years before the new Algebra I curriculum went into place, the first year of implementation (as a transitional year), and the last 2 years. She admitted, however, that she did not have the time to gather these data for all students; she would have to gather data on only a sample of the students. "I know how to use a random number table to generate a sample of students, but I'm not sure how many students would be enough." Mrs. Lasha suggested that she ask the professor of the course for some advice, and Mr. Hughes suggested that perhaps about 50 students per year might be adequate. Ms. Chinn agreed to seek advice, so the discussion turned to what correlations should be computed.

Ms. Townsend asked if there were some way to correlate the Algebra I grades with all of the other measures simultaneously, but Ms. Chinn suggested that that might mask the different effects of each of these measures in being able to predict algebra performance. "Perhaps it would be better for our purposes to correlate each of the measures separately to determine which one of them was most related to the Algebra I grade. Then we would know which of the measures might be the 'best' one to call attention to when we want to identify which students should take Algebra I." Ms. Townsend reflected that, if both types of correlations were computed (i.e., individual and collective), their understanding of the relationship among the variables would be richer. Ms. Chinn said that she would ask her professor about this problem and make the best decision that she could, given her own developing understanding of correlation procedures.

Refine Evaluation Questions

The teachers were left, however, with concerns about how many years of data they needed to gather. Mr. Hughes raised the question: "What do we really want to know?" Everyone agreed that they wanted to know which parts of their process of recommendation for algebra were actually effective in identifying the students who were most successful in algebra. Ms. Townsend reminded them that there had been an increase in the failure rate of Algebra I students, so their process used to be more effective than it was now. If they were going to change the process, they should know which parts were most likely to identify successful students. Therefore, she suggested, it might be useful to compare the 2 years prior to the implementation of the new curriculum against the 2 most recent years. After a few more minutes of discussion, the teachers agreed that this plan seemed reasonable, but they weren't sure that it was the best plan. Further, they didn't know how to find out if they had made a reasonable decision. Mr. Hughes suggested that the professor of the course might be able to help them, so Ms. Chinn agreed to add this question to the list of questions she was preparing to take to the professor.

Obtain Permission to Gather Data

At the next meeting, Ms. Chinn reported first that her professor liked the idea of comparing the 2 years prior to the implementation of the new curriculum to the 2 most recent years. Further, he agreed that gathering data on 40-50 students per year seemed like enough data and that the computer software could compute both individual and multiple correlations. The next tasks facing the teachers were gathering the data and entering it into a computer file. Ms. Chinn reiterated that she needed some help because the amount of data was quite large: 50 students per year for 4 different years, with four pieces of data for each student. Ms. Chinn also raised a question that her professor had raised: What permissions from the school district are required before the data can be gathered? Mr. Hughes said that he had anticipated this problem, so he had already approached the superintendent's office to ask about what approvals would be necessary. The superintendent said that, as long as the data were used only internally within the district, no permissions were needed. When Mr. Hughes said the Ms. Chinn wanted to use the data for her project, however, the superintendent said that the committee would have to submit a memo to the Council of Assistant Superintendents explaining how the data would be used. Mr. Hughes shared a draft of a memo that he had prepared to obtain the necessary permission, and after brief discussion the teachers agreed that it was adequate. (The assistant superintendents approved Ms. Chinn's use of the data, so this part of the evaluation process will not be followed any further.)

Mrs. Lasha and Ms. Townsend agreed to help Ms. Chinn get the necessary data, but they both asked her to help them understand the process that would be used before they began. Ms. Chinn explained that first they had to get a list of all students who took Algebra I in a given year. "Let's assume as an example that there are 230. Then we begin reading three-digit numbers in a random number table, and write down the first 50 different ones that are less than or equal to 230. These numbers identify the 50 students that we will gather data on for that year. Since the data come from the school files of the students, we will have to do this in the high school office." This explanation was adequate to get the team started, so they agreed to go to the high school office after school each day the following week to see if they could get the data they needed.

TABLE 2.1   Correlations

Variables	Years Prior to Implementation	Most Recent Years
Eighth-grade course grade & Algebra I grade	0.31	0.24
Standardized test score & Algebra I grade	0.20	0.19
Teacher recommendation & Algebra I grade	0.33	0.22
Three variables & Algebra I grade	0.35	0.27

Collecting and Analyzing the Data

It turned out that getting the lists of algebra students for the 4 years in question took more time than they expected. All they could find were individual class lists; there was no master list of algebra students. With perseverance, however, they were able to gather the necessary data in seven afternoons of work in the high school office.

Ms. Chinn then began the process of entering the data in the university computer. This took most of a Saturday. Only then was she able to begin to use SAS (a statistical analysis package) to compute the correlations. As is typical of most computer activities, the first few times she tried to run the data through SAS, there were minor mistakes in the control commands, so the results weren't actually ready to share with the other teachers until 4 weeks later.

Organizing the Data

The correlations of the variables are reported in Table 2.1. Correlations are reported for the 2 years prior to implementation of the new Algebra I curriculum and for the most recent 2 years. Both individual and multiple correlations are reported.

Interpreting the Results

Looking for Patterns in the Data

Ms. Chinn discussed the results with her professor and then reported their interpretations to the committee. The first observation she made was to point out that the correlations were all fairly small. This means that none of the parts of the recommendation process showed a particularly strong relationship with students' final grades in Algebra I. The decreasing pattern of correlations across the two time periods, however, may be considered evidence of the fact that there has been an increasing "discontinuity" between the eighth-grade mathematics course and Algebra I. That is, the pattern in the data is consistent with a hypothesis of greater discontinuity.

It is also noteworthy that, in the older data, the correlation between teacher recommendation and Algebra I grade is higher than the correlation between eighth-grade course grade and Algebra I grade, but this pattern is reversed in the more recent data. It is quite common for previous performance (e.g., grades in prerequisite courses) to correlate significantly with later performance, so we would expect that there would be a correlation between eighth-grade course grades and Algebra I grades. The fact, however, that eighth-grade teachers seem less effective at identifying successful students in Algebra I again supports the hypothesis that the discontinuity is growing between the courses.

The correlations for the standardized test scores seem to be holding fairly steady at a low level. The standardized test used in eighth grade does not seem very useful at identifying the successful Algebra I students. Also, the fact that the multiple correlations are higher than any of the individual correlations is expected, because more of the information is represented in those statistics.

Using the Information

The next problem facing the teachers was how to make use of the information that they had gathered. The initial discussion centered on the fact that the correlations of teacher recommendation had declined the most. Ms. Townsend said that she really wanted her recommendations to be accurate, and, if they were not as accurate now, then she would look for ways to make them better. She also admitted, however, that she would likely need some help in knowing what to focus on differently. Mrs. Lasha agreed that they would all probably need help in this area.

Improving Teacher Recommendation

Mr. Hughes then raised the question of what they thought would happen to the correlations if the eighth-grade course were changed. Mrs. Lasha suggested that the correlations between performance in the eighth-grade course and Algebra I should increase if the two courses were more consistent. Similarly, if the teachers were careful in watching the performance of their students on problems and exercises similar to those used in Algebra I, then they should be able to make better recommendations about which students were likely to be successful. Ms. Chinn said that this latter effort would require that the teachers understand what the new Algebra I course was like. "Would it be possible for us to have a workshop on the content of the new Algebra I curriculum? If so, should we have that workshop together with the high school algebra teachers?" Mr. Hughes said that he liked the idea of meeting with the high school teachers. "Maybe if we all had a common background about what algebra content was important to teach, we could help the students make a more successful transition from middle school to high school." He also noted that he thought that requests for workshops would bring a positive reaction from the district's mathematics coordinator, but he wondered if there were other topics that teachers could suggest for useful workshops. Mrs. Lasha and Ms. Townsend said they would like to have time to think about this question, so the remainder of the discussion of this issue was put off until the next meeting.

At the next meeting, the teachers discussed a variety of issues to which they had given thought. Included in the list were assessment of algebra performance, new content that might need to be included in the eighth-grade course, alternative standardized tests that might better reflect a revised curriculum, development of problem-solving skills, motivation of middle school students, and so on. Two of the teachers suggested that it might be useful to have input from the high school teachers in planning a revised eighth-grade curriculum so that students would have an easier transition. The major task of the teachers now is to prioritize the list of topics and make a request of the district for assistance.

Developing Continuity Between Middle School and High School

Students are likely to achieve more if there is continuity in academic programs as students move from one level to the next (e.g., elementary school to middle school, middle school to high school). This is especially true, however, during periods of rapid educational reform when teachers at each level are likely to make changes without having time to obtain carefully considered feedback from teachers at other levels. It is important that students not get caught in the "cross fire" and be expected to perform without having adequate preparation for changing expectations. School personnel can avoid many of the pitfalls of reform if communication can be opened and maintained among teachers and administrators across different grade levels. This communication takes effort, but it has an important payoff for student performance.

Mr. Hughes developed a memo that summarized the evaluation efforts of the teachers. The memo addressed the purpose and focus of the evaluation, the steps followed to complete the evaluation, the results, and the recommendations for action. The memo was sent to the principals at the middle school and high school, and copies were sent to all the mathematics teachers at both schools.

Summary of Evaluation Principles

This vignette illustrates several important principles that should be kept in mind in evaluations of school programs.

1. Do not attempt to evaluate every aspect of a program at once. Focus the evaluation by selecting a few indicators of quality. There are many possible reasons that students might be increasingly unsuccessful in Algebra I. Focusing on the recommendation process allowed the eighth-grade teachers to begin to examine the relationship of their own practices to the long-term success of their students. Further, it focused their attention on ways that they might provide better help to their students.

2. When choosing a method of data collection, try to select an alternative that minimizes the burden on those who will be asked to provide information. All the relevant information for the evaluation was contained in the school's files, so there was no need to generate further information from either students or teachers. Because this information was not organized specifically for the purpose of this evaluation, the only burden on the teachers was that of gathering the information and putting it into a computer file that could be accessed by the SAS software.

3. Whenever possible, collect information in ways that give every member of the group of interest an opportunity to participate. Remember that you will typically want to draw conclusions about the performance of all students, opinions of all teachers, judgments of all parents, and so on. The decision to sample from among all Algebra I students was made to keep the data set manageable. The use of a random sample allowed appropriate conclusions to be drawn for the larger population.

4. Collect information that will help to identify areas of program strength and weakness and to guide remedial action when improvement is needed. Because the teachers were not instructors of Algebra I, they could not directly control the content or the presentation of the concepts and skills of that course. Because they were responsible for preparing students to take that course, however, it was important for them to understand the effects of their recommendation practices. As they became aware that they might not be recommending students in the most appropriate way, they were led to discuss alternatives to those practices. Further follow-up on the effects of changes in practices would be necessary as the teachers continued to monitor their work with students.

5. Whenever possible, seek redundant information. Ask several questions about each important evaluation issue. The use of multiple sources of information for placing students in Algebra I is an excellent model. Understanding the differential effects of each of these measures is important if teachers are to know what the best instructional practices are to be.

Alternatives to the Strategy Used Here

Given that most of the indicators for the algebra standard are phrased in terms of opportunities for students to develop understanding, student data were the obvious kind of information for assessing the indicators. Interviews of students also might have revealed information about why students were failing Algebra I at a higher rate, but gathering such information is very time consuming, and it would have been impossible to locate enough students from previous years to obtain a multiyear perspective on the problem. Another reason to reject this method of data collection was the fact that interviewers can often provide students with helpful hints, without meaning to, simply in the manner they choose to ask questions or use their voices. Teachers are so used to teaching rather than interviewing that it is sometimes difficult for them just to listen to what students know without at the same time trying to improve or "fix" that understanding.

The middle school teachers also might have attacked their problem by asking the high school teachers what should be taught in the eighth-grade mathematics course. The high school teachers could surely comment on the "mathematical prerequisites" of Algebra I, but those teachers might not understand very well what young adolescents were capable of learning and might not recognize the limitations of the knowledge base of eighth-grade students. This approach might be a useful follow-up technique for the middle school teachers as a check on whether the appropriate mathematics concepts were being included in the revised eighth-grade course.

Cautions Regarding Misinterpretation

The correlations that were computed in the evaluation are rather low. This means that only a small part of the variance in the data is being accounted for by the variables being examined, so there probably are other variables that are important to consider. Further reflection on the process of student placement in Algebra I seems to be needed to fully understand the complexity of the process and the ways that variables interact with each other.

As indicated earlier, the obvious conclusion drawn by the evaluation team was that the students at Lincoln Middle were not being provided with the educational opportunities necessary to allow a smooth transition from arithmetic into algebra. Changing the eighth-grade program, however, is not without its risks. A more complete analysis of the discontinuity between the eighth-grade curriculum and the Algebra I curriculum would be in order as the changes are contemplated. Teachers will have to deal with placement decisions when information on a particular student is inconsistent. For example, when the eighth-grade course grade is high and the standardized test score is low, what is the best decision to make about placement in Algebra I? What happens when the grade and score are moderately high but the teacher does not provide a strong recommendation? We hope that, before concluding this self-evaluation study, members of the faculty will seek answers to these questions.

3 Vignette Three

Manipulative Resources for Instruction

Instruction Builds on What Students Already Know

All students, and especially elementary school students, bring considerable intuitive knowledge with them to school. This knowledge is typically based on their interactions with the world around them and is often generalized from manipulation of objects in their environment. Much of this knowledge is useful as a basis for helping students develop understanding of mathematics concepts, but the task of making mathematics instruction consistent with what children know about the world is not easy. Recent national reports on the state of mathematics education recognize the need to connect mathematics instruction to the real world; for elementary school students, these connections can be made partly through the use of various manipulatives during the time that concepts are being taught. Use of manipulatives also has the advantage that it will often sustain both the interest of students in learning about mathematics and their positive attitudes about mathematics. Many teachers now recognize the need to incorporate manipulatives in instruction, but they don't always have the resources in their buildings to carry out that instruction.

Where, What, and Why?

Mitchell Elementary School is 2 years old. Built in one of the city's affluent suburbs, it draws students primarily from high-income professional families. There are 750 students in kindergarten through Grade 5. Many students are brought to school in the mornings by parents who commute into the city, while others have short bus rides of 20-30 minutes. Mitchell's after-school day-care program has been a tremendous success as parents take advantage of the opportunity to pick their children up on their way home from work. Most of the parents are college educated or have received professional training from 2-year institutions and are interested and involved in the education of their children. Even though Mitchell is not well balanced socioeconomically, racially its students are quite diverse: About 45% are white, about 45% are black, and about 10% are from other minority groups.

Principals Provide Key Instructional Leadership

Ellen Drew has been principal of Mitchell since its doors first opened. Having become a principal in 1986, Dr. Drew played a prominent role in the planning, supervision, and decision making necessary during the entire construction period for Mitchell. She looks at Mitchell almost as would a proud parent and is determined that her school will be among those touted as the best in the state. Dr. Drew was very careful in selection of the faculty and staff members. She often comments that her state-of-the-art building deserves a state-of-the-art faculty, so, in addition to the 20 teachers, there is 1 counselor, 1 media specialist, 1 half-time nurse, and 2 secretaries. Of the 20 teachers, 8 hold master's degrees, 2 were teachers-of-the-year at their former buildings, and 3 hold advanced certificates. Dr. Drew works hard and expects the same commitment from her staff. Because Mitchell's teachers regard Dr. Drew as fair, supportive, and willing to listen, they support her and approve of her vision for their school. She has won the respect of the surrounding community and is well liked by the students.

The state's curriculum, however, has historically been driven by the choice of standardized tests used at Grades 2, 4, and 6 to assess what students know. During the past decade, one company has had the state contract for providing the tests and analyzing the results. That test has been oriented toward computational skills and recognition of terminology, with little attention given to understanding of concepts or to significant problem solving. Recently, however, the state education agency rewrote the mathematics curriculum framework so that it is more in line with the *Curriculum and Evaluation Standards for School Mathematics* (NCTM, 1989). The new framework strongly suggests that mathematics instruction in elementary and middle schools should involve the use of manipulatives in the development of both conceptual understanding and problem-solving skills.

Teachers Provide Key Instructional Leadership

Because of the leadership of Dr. Drew in developing Mitchell's strong academic program that is recognized throughout the state, Mrs. Cahali, a third-grade teacher, participated in the writing and editing of the elementary school section of the new mathematics framework. Mrs. Cahali has become a leader in helping the other teachers at Mitchell think about the quality of their mathematics instruction. She has attended three regional meetings of the National Council of Teachers of Mathematics, where she has been introduced to many different ideas about the use of manipulatives in teaching mathematics. She recognizes that the *Standards* reflects a new philosophy about mathematics instruction, but she also realizes that it would be difficult to implement all aspects of that philosophy simultaneously. Based on her discussions with other members of the writing team for the new state framework, she believes that implementation of the use of manipulatives in instruction is the most obvious place to begin what might ultimately turn out to be an entire realignment of the curriculum to match the new framework.

At the start of the current school year, she suggested to Dr. Drew that it might be profitable for the teachers to organize a discussion group (or focus group) to consider how effectively their curriculum is taking advantage of the power of manipulatives in helping students develop deep understanding of mathematics concepts. Because Mitchell has a history of having groups of teachers discuss and evaluate their efforts and then make suggestions for improvements, Dr. Drew readily agreed and asked Mrs. Cahali to act as chair of the group. Seven teachers agreed to work with Mrs. Cahali on this task.

As the state school board leaves the specification of exact standards and indicators up to each district, the first task facing the committee was deciding how to implement the new state framework. Mrs. Cahali said that one of the helpful documents that the state writing team had during the last round of editing was *Mathematics Programs: A Guide to Evaluation*, which was part of a set of content guides recently published by Corwin Press. She showed her copy of the guide to the committee and called their attention to the standards and indicators in Resource A in that guide. The committee compared those standards with the state's framework and agreed that the match was fairly close, so they asked Mrs. Cahali to contact the district's mathematics coordinator to see if these standards and indicators would be acceptable to the district as Mitchell's first approximation of creating a context for their mathematics curriculum. The committee agreed to meet again in 2 weeks.

At the next committee meeting, Mrs. Cahali reported that the mathematics coordinator had reviewed the standards and indicators in the guide and said that they would be acceptable for initial consideration of possible changes in the curriculum at Mitchell. Mr. Poliga, a second-grade teacher, suggested that it might be profitable for

Mrs. Cahali to summarize the deliberations of the writing team for the new framework so that the changes at Mitchell will continue to keep the school at the forefront of statewide improvements in mathematics instruction.

Curriculum Initiatives: Problem Solving and Manipulatives

Mrs. Cahali first noted that the work of the writing team was very difficult; there were many different philosophies of team members that had to be assimilated by the entire team. The two changes that primarily became the focus of discussion, however, were problem solving and manipulatives. Over the course of the writing, each of the team members reported on the efforts of their districts to enhance the teaching of problem-solving and thinking skills. The overall impression left by these discussions was that, when teachers had a good sense of how to use manipulatives, the inservice on problem solving seemed to be more easily implemented in the curriculum. Mrs. Cahali reported that it was these impressions that had led her to suggest the formation of this committee. She further speculated that it might have been a lack of use of manipulatives that had led to an incomplete implementation of the problem-solving ideas that had been presented in workshops held at Mitchell last year.

Ms. Frango and Ms. Zinta supported Mrs. Cahali's views by commenting that their use of geometry problem-solving activities were not successful because they had not been able to get the children beyond the stage of "playing with" the pattern blocks. Until now, they hadn't given any thought to the possibility that the difficulty may have stemmed from their own unfamiliarity with the use of those manipulatives. But, because that was the first time they had tried to use those manipulatives in instruction, such an argument made considerable sense.

The discussion then turned to consideration of what "appropriate use of manipulatives" might mean. Mr. Poliga said that, from his reading of the NCTM's *Standards,* it seemed like manipulatives were most useful for modeling mathematical ideas to students, "especially after they have some exposure to those ideas." Ms. Frango, however, took a slightly different view. "It seems to me that students need to use manipulatives when they are introduced to an idea. Manipulatives seem to help provide a visual situation which students can more easily remember later on." Mrs. Cahali commented that the descriptions provided during the framework writing committee spanned a wide range of uses. "Some of the stories were descriptions of use of manipulatives during the initial teaching of an idea, but some uses didn't happen until students had already learned some things about the ideas. In those cases, the use of manipulatives almost seemed to be a summary of what had been learned. I think manipulatives can be used effectively in many different ways."

Defining Terms   The discussion continued for almost an hour. The teachers seemed to be trying to negotiate a common understanding of the idea of "manipulatives" so that they could move on to the task of deciding what information they wanted to know about the use of manipulatives at Mitchell Elementary. Finally, Ms. Frango said, "We've been using the word 'manipulative' as if we all understood it in the same way. Perhaps it is important for us to agree on some of the characteristics of manipulatives so that we could then decide what information we want to gather." This comment caused a pause in the conversation, after which three of the teachers spoke almost at the same time. Mrs. Cahali intervened to bring order to the discussion and then went to the chalkboard to write down the characteristics that were suggested, along with an example of a manipulative that possessed each characteristic. "Let's first brainstorm to get a list. Then we'll go back over the list to see if we agree with each of the characteristics."

- models a mathematical idea (e.g., base 10 blocks)
- helps visualize an idea (e.g., cardboard clocks)
- provides an aid to memory (e.g., paper and pencil)
- helps to gather data about objects (e.g., rulers)
- models a real-world event (e.g., play money)
- generates information related to an idea (e.g., dice)

At this point, the discussion seemed to run out of steam. Mrs. Cahali asked if there were any items in the list with which anyone was uncomfortable. Two teachers said they didn't like to think of "paper and pencil" as a manipulative, and three others agreed. Ms. Zinta asked if removing this characteristic would also remove calculators from consideration. Mr. Poliga said that he used calculators for more than a memory aid. "I ask students to explore patterns with their calculators. Isn't this more than a memory aid?" When Ms. Frango asked if the students could do the computations without the calculator, Mr. Poliga responded that he thought so, but it would take a lot more time, and there might be lots of errors in the computations. "Students might lose sight of the pattern if they spent all their energy on doing the computations." Ms. Frango then observed that this sounded like the calculator was simply an aid to their mental powers. "In that sense, it seems like the calculator is more like an aid to memory than a model for the mathematical ideas." All of the other teachers agreed that they had not thought about this issue before, but they were leaning toward the view that calculators, although very important to implementation of a quality mathematics curriculum, should not be considered as a manipulative. The teachers than settled on the remaining five characteristics as important parts of the idea of manipulatives, though they agreed that other characteristics might have to be added later:

Multiple Perspectives

- models a mathematical idea (e.g., base 10 blocks)
- helps visualize an idea (e.g., cardboard clocks)
- helps to gather data about objects (e.g., rulers)
- models a real-world event (e.g., play money)
- generates information related to an idea (e.g., dice)

Focusing the Evaluation

The discussion turned to deciding what aspects of the use of manipulatives should become the focus of the evaluation. Several ideas were quickly suggested: how often teachers used manipulatives in teaching, how often students used manipulatives, what topics were taught with manipulatives, how long manipulatives were used in the development of a concept, and what manipulative use was suggested by the textbook series. At this point, however, Ms. Frango asked, "Do we have the right manipulatives in our building? If not, then it might be futile to continue to talk about how other manipulatives are being used." This comment caused the committee to stop. Mrs. Cahali commented that Ms. Frango had indeed identified a critical point in their deliberations.

She asked if anyone on the committee had a good idea of what manipulatives were available to use. The committee started to list what they had used recently: base 10 blocks, rulers, pattern blocks, dice. Ms. Zinta asked, "Even though we are listing manipulatives that we have used, do we know how many of each type are available? And probably more important, do we know which manipulatives we are supposed to be using?" Ms. Frango added, "How could we decide what manipulatives we should be using?" Mr. Poliga said that he thought these questions were really at the heart of their considerations. He suggested that they spend some time discussing them.

What Kinds of Manipulatives Do Teachers Need?

Mrs. Cahali suggested that they begin with the last question: How could the committee decide what manipulatives they needed? Ms. Frango suggested that they look through the standards and indicators to identify all of the indicators that mentioned the use of manipulatives. The indicators that they found are listed below:

2. Mathematics as Communication
  2.1. Students have opportunities to relate physical materials, pictures, and diagrams to mathematical ideas, with increasing emphasis on graphing and algebraic methods as the students mature.
4. Mathematical Connections
  4.4. Students have opportunities to explore and describe results using graphic, numerical, physical, algebraic, and verbal models or representations.

14. Learning Environment

    14.7. Teachers are given an inventory of available manipulatives (e.g., geoboards) and supplementary instructional materials (e.g., videotapes); materials in adequate variety and sufficient quantity are easily accessible; materials are matched with the instructional program; and materials are used by students in learning.

    14.8. Equipment (e.g., calculators, computers, overhead projectors, and so on) to support the mathematics program is readily available and securely stored.

18. Alignment

    18.2. Student assessments are aligned with the goals, objectives, and mathematical content of the curriculum and with instructional approaches (e.g., use of calculators, computers, and manipulatives) used by teachers.

    18.3. Teaching practices include use of different grouping strategies (i.e., large group, small group, individual) and appropriate manipulatives and technologies.

Collecting Preliminary Information

Outside Resources
    The listing of these indicators left the committee somewhat confused, because the indicators often did not specify what manipulatives might be appropriate. Ms. Zinta suggested that perhaps they might have to examine the content standards to see what manipulatives might be appropriate for use. Ms. Frango said that she didn't want their thinking to be limited just to their own knowledge of manipulatives, but she wasn't sure what resources would be helpful to them in breaking out of their own experience to include manipulatives with which they might not be familiar. Mrs. Cahali said that the writing team had found elementary mathematics methods books to be a useful source of information on what manipulatives could be used in teaching. They agreed that the first four standards were so general that any manipulatives might be used to implement them. It was the specific conceptual content that they needed to review. The committee members agreed to divide content Standards 5 through 11 among themselves, with each person being responsible for one of the standards. Each person would review at least three elementary methods books (available from their personal resources, the teachers' resource room, or the local university library), along with some of the issues of *The Arithmetic Teacher* in the teachers' resource room at Mitchell, and make a list of manipulatives that would seem to be useful to teach the standard. The committee agreed to complete this task within 3 weeks.

Using the Information Collected

Mrs. Cahali raised the question of what they would do with this information. Mr. Poliga suggested that once they knew what manipulatives were appropriate for use, then they might do a survey of what manipulatives were available in the building so that they could find out what support was available for teachers and what new purchases might be needed. The new purchase list could be given to Dr. Drew so that she could build those purchases into the long-range plan for the building. He further suggested that, if there were an adequate supply of manipulatives in the building, the committee might be able to suggest to Dr. Drew a series of topics for inservice workshops to help the teachers learn how to take advantage of those existing resources. The committee agreed that this seemed like a good plan, but someone would have to plan a method of gathering the information for the building. Mrs. Cahali volunteered to suggest a method to use if someone would help her. Ms. Zinta volunteered to help.

Planning the Data Gathering Process

Inventory Procedures

Mrs. Cahali and Ms. Zinta met the next week to brainstorm about how they might get information about the manipulatives that were in the building. After a few minutes of discussion, they focused on two possible techniques: (a) have one person or a team of people look in every classroom and every closet in the building to catalog all the manipulatives or (b) have each teacher catalog the manipulatives in her or his classroom and closets. The advantage of the first technique would be that the team might be more careful about listing all the manipulatives. Clearly, however, this approach would require the committee to invest a lot of time. Conversely, the advantage of the second technique is that the effort would be distributed over a larger number of people. But the committee would not be as sure that all of the manipulatives would be accurately counted. They decided that the better use of time would be to ask each teacher to do a classroom inventory, with the committee taking the responsibility for checking the closets in "common" areas of the building, like the learning resource center, the teachers' resource room, and so on.

They then discussed the structure of the form that they would give to teachers. The simplest form would be just a listing of all the manipulatives that the committee agreed were appropriate, with space provided by each item for teachers to write down how many of that manipulative were in the room. There would also be space at the bottom of the form for teachers to list other manipulatives that they had available in their rooms.

Further Planning

When the committee met again, each teacher had a list of manipulatives that they had identified in their review of both the elementary mathematics methods books and the mathematics instructional journals. Mrs. Cahali made a combined list on the blackboard:

5. Number, Numeration, and Computation
   Cuisenaire rods, base 10 blocks, chip trading materials, play money, abacus, fraction and decimal models, fraction bars, number line for wall display
6. Patterns and Functions
   pattern blocks, attribute pieces, buttons, number balance
7. Measurement
   rulers, tape measures, area models (e.g., square inch, square foot, square yard, square centimeter, square decimeter, square meter), grid paper (metric and customary sizes), volume measures, protractor, double pan balances, weights (metric and customary), cardboard clocks, thermometers
8. Statistics and Data Analysis
   graph paper of various sizes
9. Geometry and Spatial Reasoning
   two-dimensional shapes, three-dimensional shapes, rulers, protractors, square and triangular grid paper, geoboards
10. Algebra
    graph paper, pattern materials (e.g., pattern blocks)
11. Probability and Discrete Mathematics
    dice, spinners, graph paper

Manipulatives and Technology

Mr. Poliga then raised the question of whether computer software should be included in the list. Ms. Zinta argued that computers ought to be included in the list because computer tools could create information that could be manipulated mentally. One of the books that she consulted had made a strong argument that the images created by computers were very useful in helping children develop skills at manipulating information mentally. This comment led to a lively discussion that lasted for almost a half hour. Some teachers expressed concern that there were so few computers in the building and that teachers had had so little inservice in the use of computers that a survey might not yield useful information. That is, many of the teachers would respond that they didn't have computers or computer software to use, but this information would not be very helpful for planning changes, just because the teachers had so little knowledge of what software was appropriate for children to use. At the end of the discussion, the committee agreed that, over the next couple of years, it would be important for their mathematics instruction to move toward integration of computers in instruction, but the survey right now should not deal with this issue. Another focus group might be needed in about a year to make suggestions for moving Mitchell Elementary forward in the use of technology.

Choosing Among Competing Viewpoints

Mr. Poliga again raised the question of inclusion of calculators. "One of the books I read said outright that calculators were a manipulative, and one said that they weren't. I'm not sure what position we should take." Ms. Frango thought that calculators should not be included. "In spite of the fact that one of the books took the opposite view, I think that our earlier decision is correct. Calculators seem to primarily support extensions of mental powers to make work easier. Manipulatives need to do more than this." Ms. Zinta thought that, because calculators were so important to mathematics teaching, they should be included in the survey. "Maybe we can kill two birds with one stone and find out how many calculators are in the building." Mrs. Cahali suggested that to include calculators on a survey of manipulatives might leave the teachers with the impression that calculators are a manipulative. "This may be the wrong message to send." Mr. Poliga said that he basically agreed with Mrs. Cahali. "Even though calculators are important, we should deal with the technology issue separately." After a few more minutes of discussion, the teachers agreed that the manipulatives survey should deal only with manipulatives and that they should recommend to Dr. Drew that another focus group be organized soon to deal with the technology issue.

Mrs. Cahali then presented the plan for gathering data for the building. She showed them a prototype of the survey form (Figure 3.1) with the comment, based on the work that the teachers had reported at this meeting, that the list of manipulatives was obviously incomplete. The prototype survey form was developed only to show what it would look like. The task of expanding the list of manipulatives would be an easy one. Mr. Poliga commented that he often wished that he had overhead versions of manipulatives to use for demonstrations. "Should we include a column for reporting on overhead versions of manipulatives?" Everyone agreed that this would yield important information, so it was added as the second column. Ms. Frango wondered out loud whether all of the teachers would know the names of all of the manipulatives. She suggested that perhaps there should be a third column that allowed each teacher to say that he or she didn't know what a particular manipulative looked like. The committee agreed that this was a great addition to the survey and would reduce the chance that the wrong objects would be counted. The completed survey is presented in Figure 3.2.

Manipulatives in Mitchell

Room: _____

Manipulative	*Number available*
base 10 blocks	_____
dice	_____
rulers	_____
other (please specify)	_____
_____	_____
_____	_____
_____	_____

Figure 3.1. Prototype Survey Form

Conducting the Survey

The committee agreed that the revised survey form was appropriate, so they began a discussion of when it should be sent out, how long the teachers should have to complete it, who on the committee would look in the "common" areas of the building, and so on. After a short discussion, they agreed that the survey form should go out within the next 2 weeks but that it should be sent from Dr. Drew with a cover memo explaining the need for the information and asking for the cooperation of all the teachers. The committee further agreed that the teachers should have 2 weeks to return the results and that the completed surveys should be returned to Mrs. Cahali, as chair of the committee. Ms. Frango and Ms. Zinta agreed to check all of the common areas in addition to their classrooms to be sure that the list of manipulatives was complete. Finally, the committee asked Mrs. Cahali to take their plans to Dr. Drew to elicit her cooperation in conducting the survey.

Organizing the Results

Mrs. Cahali met the next week with Dr. Drew to discuss the work of the committee and the plans for the survey. Dr. Drew complimented the committee on how thorough they had been in identifying manipulatives that were potentially useful for the teaching of mathematics and readily agreed to write the cover memo for the survey. She said that her review of the new state framework for mathematics instruction had raised in her mind a concern about whether Mitchell's teachers were using manipulatives extensively enough. She admitted that she had not given much thought to the question of whether there were enough manipulatives, or manipulatives of the right kind, in the building, so this survey ought to provide very useful information for the

Manipulatives in Mitchell

Room: _____

Directions: Please determine whether you have a classroom set of each type of manipulative in your room and in the storage areas. If you don't know what a particular name refers to, please check the "I don't know" column. Thank you for your help in gathering this information.

Manipulative	Classroom set available for students	Overhead demonstration versions	I don't know
Cuisenaire rods	_____	_____	_____
base 10 blocks	_____	_____	_____
chip trading materials	_____	_____	_____
play money	_____	_____	_____
abacus	_____	_____	_____
fraction/decimal models	_____	_____	_____
fraction bars	_____	_____	_____
number line for wall display	_____	_____	_____
pattern blocks	_____	_____	_____
attribute pieces	_____	_____	_____
buttons and other counting objects	_____	_____	_____
number balance	_____	_____	_____
rulers	_____	_____	_____
tape measures	_____	_____	_____
area models (e.g., square inch, square foot, square yard, square centimeter, square decimeter, square meter)			
metric grid paper	_____	_____	_____
customary grid paper	_____	_____	_____
volume measures	_____	_____	_____
protractors	_____	_____	_____
double pan balances	_____	_____	_____
weights (metric and customary)	_____	_____	_____
cardboard clocks	_____	_____	_____
thermometers	_____	_____	_____
two-dimensional shapes	_____	_____	_____
three-dimensional shapes	_____	_____	_____
square and triangular grid paper	_____	_____	_____
geoboards	_____	_____	_____
dice	_____	_____	_____
spinners	_____	_____	
other: _____	_____	_____	
_____	_____	_____	

Figure 3.2. Completed Survey Form

teachers in their planning of the mathematics curriculum. Dr. Drew asked, however, if the committee had made any plans for sharing the information with other teachers at Mitchell. Mrs. Cahali admitted that they had not, but she agreed to take this concern to the committee at its next meeting.

Follow-Up of Nonrespondents

Dr. Drew sent out the forms the following week, asking the teachers to return their completed forms to Mrs. Cahali. At the end of the 2-week period, Mrs. Cahali had received 16 completed forms. This meant that four teachers had not yet completed their inventories. Mrs. Cahali identified these four teachers by checking the room numbers listed on the completed forms and was able to get their information after she visited with each one of the teachers to explain how important the survey was for the future development of the mathematics curriculum for Mitchell. Mrs. Cahali compiled all teachers' responses (Figure 3.3). She also called another meeting of the committee.

Interpreting the Results

At the next committee meeting, Mrs. Cahali asked for a report on what had been found in the common areas so that the committee would have a complete picture of the availability of manipulatives. Ms. Frango and Ms. Zinta reported that they had found very few manipulatives in the common areas. "We found enough fraction models for a couple of classrooms, a dozen geoboards, and four double pan balances with weights." Mrs. Cahali asked the teachers to add this information to their copies of the summary of teachers' responses.

Resources Need to Support All Areas of Instruction

Then the teachers launched into a discussion of the results. The first thing they noticed was that there were some gaps in the available manipulatives at Mitchell, most notably fraction models, some measuring tools, geometry materials, and probability tools. They seemed to have enough sets of manipulatives, however, for whole number concepts, simple measuring, and graphic representations. Ms. Frango asked how they might decide how many manipulatives would be enough for a particular content strand. Ms. Zinta reminded them that the new state curriculum framework had very similar strands for each grade level; for example, number concepts, geometry, statistics. "The grade level differences in manipulatives may be related more to differences in the level of sophistication of each concept across grade levels than to the differences in coverage of content across grades." Mrs. Cahali agreed that the reforms in mathematics instruction seemed to be calling for more manipulatives to be used in more grade levels. "If we are going to be successful at implementing the state framework, each

Manipulatives in Mitchell (Counts by Classrooms)

Room: _____

Directions: Please determine whether you have a classroom set of each type of manipulative in your room and in the storage areas. If you don't know what a particular name refers to, please check the "I don't know" column. Thank you for your help in gathering this information.

Manipulative	*Classroom set available for students*	*Overhead demonstration versions*	*I don't know*
Cuisenaire rods	14	2	3
base 10 blocks	12	0	_____
chip trading materials	2	0	9
play money	17	3	_____
abacus	1	0	_____
fraction/decimal models	7	2	_____
fraction bars	3	2	_____
number line for wall display	14	NA	_____
pattern blocks	6	0	8
attribute pieces	0	0	16
buttons and other counting objects	19	8	_____
number balance	5	NA	_____
rulers	16	0	_____
tape measures	12	NA	_____
area models (e.g., square inch, square foot, square yard, square centimeter, square decimeter, square meter)	3	1	_____
metric grid paper	1	1	_____
customary grid paper	4	2	_____
volume measures	5	NA	_____
protractors	10	7	_____
double pan balances	3	NA	_____
weights (metric and customary)	3	NA	_____
cardboard clocks	5	NA	_____
thermometers	2	NA	_____
two-dimensional shapes	8	2	_____
three-dimensional shapes	6	NA	_____
square and triangular grid paper	9	1	_____
geoboards	4	2	6
dice	7	NA	_____
spinners	3	1	_____
other: _____	_____	_____	
_____	_____	_____	

Figure 3.3. Survey Results

teacher needs to have ready access to manipulatives. Perhaps we should think of our classrooms as laboratories for doing mathematics. Each teacher needs access to proper laboratory tools for conducting mathematical experiments." This analogy sparked additional discussion, but finally the teachers agreed that their first recommendation to Dr. Drew would be that she needed to purchase materials needed to fill the gaps in the current inventory of mathematics manipulatives.

Another obvious deficiency in available equipment was the lack of overhead versions of the manipulatives for use in instruction. Many teachers find it useful to be able to model ways that the manipulatives can be used effectively or to let the children themselves model uses of the manipulatives. This is often done most easily when overhead versions are available so that all the children can see how the manipulatives are being used. The committee agreed to ask Dr. Drew to be sure the overhead versions were ordered for teachers to use.

Teacher Workshops May Be Needed to Assure Use of Resources

Mr. Poliga then asked what follow-up recommendations ought to be made. "It seems reasonable to expect that teachers do not know much about the use of manipulatives that they don't have. But can we be sure that they know how to use the manipulatives that they do have in their classrooms?" Ms. Zinta said that she personally didn't feel very secure about how to use manipulatives effectively, so she thought that a variety of workshops on all of the manipulatives might be needed for teachers to teach mathematics more effectively. Most of the teachers on the committee agreed with this position. They all said they had been exposed to ways to use manipulatives, but they certainly didn't feel expert at using many of them. The committee agreed, then, also to suggest to Dr. Drew that a series of workshops on how to use both available and newly purchased manipulatives would probably be useful for the teachers of Mitchell Elementary. For a few more minutes, they discussed what the specific topics of these inservice sessions might be. Their first few ideas dealt with understanding what mathematics concepts could be modeled by specific manipulatives. Then they added the notion that manipulatives could be used to teach problem solving. Mrs. Cahali agreed to give these ideas to Dr. Drew.

Sharing the Evaluation Results

Mrs. Cahali then presented Dr. Drew's concern for sharing the information with the other teachers. The committee discussed this concern for a few minutes and agreed that it would be easiest to do this at a faculty meeting. Mrs. Cahali agreed to work with Dr. Drew to arrange for this sharing at a future faculty meeting.

Using the Results

Mrs. Cahali asked Ms. Frango and Mr. Poliga to present the survey results and interpretations at the next faculty meeting, scheduled for 2 weeks later. Ms. Frango asked if the teachers who had particular manipulatives, for example, geoboards, might be asked to share with the faculty ways that they have used those manipulatives to teach mathematics. "That way we can talk about the results of our survey and do some initial inservice, or at least consciousness raising, at the same time." Mrs. Cahali agreed to ask two or three teachers to do mini-demonstrations at the faculty meeting.

Develop Backup Plans

Mrs. Cahali then asked whether they should suggest a process for assuring that manipulatives were equitably distributed across classes. "If we can't get classroom sets for every teacher, how do we assure that each teacher has at least some access?" Ms. Frango suggested that they might store manipulatives in the common areas and ask teachers to check them out. Ms. Zinta responded that sometimes she didn't know in advance which manipulatives would be most useful for children to have. "Sometimes, I have to adapt a lesson on the spot and it is essential that I have the right manipulative in my closet so I can pull it out when I need it. I can't run down the hall at those times to check out what I need. It is important to have the materials in my room." Two other teachers supported this view. Mr. Poliga suggested that, if Dr. Drew didn't have enough money to buy all the manipulatives that were needed, perhaps the Parent Teacher Organization could be asked to donate some support money to purchase additional materials. Mrs. Cahali asked, however, if there were any manipulatives that might be used infrequently enough so that they could be purchased in smaller quantities and shared among classes. Ms. Frango suggested that the more sophisticated measuring equipment like double pan balances and thermometers might fit into this category. Mr. Poliga suggested that geoboards might also fit. "If students needed to unexpectedly deal with geometry concepts and geoboards were not available, we could have them use dot paper or graph paper to help understand shapes." After more discussion, the committee agreed that, if money turned out to be a problem for purchasing materials, then Mrs. Cahali could suggest to Dr. Drew that some sharing of resources might be possible.

Summary of Evaluation Principles

This vignette illustrates several important principles that should be kept in mind during all evaluations of school programs.

1. Do not attempt to evaluate every aspect of a program at once. Focus the evaluation by selecting a few indicators of quality, and take the time necessary to identify the most appropriate indicators. The committee's initial discussion included consideration of a broad area of concern: How can we keep our program at the forefront of excellent programs in the state? Their brainstorming session led to the identification of the most fundamental issue, but the process took some time. It was the insight of one of the teachers on the committee that effectively focused the deliberations of the committee: Do we have the equipment necessary to deliver quality mathematics instruction? Individual insights are often important for focusing an evaluation, so input from a variety of people is important.

2. When choosing a method of data collection, try to select an alternative that minimizes the burden on those who will be asked to provide the information. Mrs. Cahali and Ms. Zinta decided that it was easiest to get the help of all teachers at Mitchell so that the information could be gathered quickly. They decided that the potential trade-off on accuracy of information was not as significant a concern, given the nature of the data to be collected.

3. Ask questions that your information providers are able to answer, and avoid questions that require speculation. The listing of manipulatives on the survey form provided teachers with a clear indication of the information that was needed. All they had to do was count the manipulatives. Allowing teachers the option of indicating that they did not know about any of the particular manipulatives reduced the possibility that the teachers might count something other than what was listed.

4. Collect information that will help to identify areas of program strength and weakness and to guide remedial action when improvement is needed. The committee identified two areas of primary concern: first, identifying manipulatives that would be appropriate for the standards and indicators in the guide and, second, identifying which of these manipulatives were available for Mitchell's teachers to use. They assumed the responsibility of dealing with the first of these concerns, but they got all of the teachers involved in dealing with the second. The major deficiency in their plan would seem to be that they developed no mechanism for getting the information into the hands of the teachers. Dr. Drew was able to point out this concern and the committee had a chance to remedy it.

5. Gather data that will lead to appropriate action. The teachers considered whether to gather information about computer software, but they decided that this information might sidetrack the teachers in the building by diverting attention from the main focus of the evaluation. It is common to want to try to gather data on many different aspects of a problem. But sometimes the additional data interfere with making appropriate decisions to solve the problem at hand.

Alternatives to the Strategy Used Here

There are many alternative ways to evaluate the suitability and use of manipulatives in the building. First, teachers could be asked to list the manipulatives in their rooms on a sheet of paper. The main disadvantage of this approach is that teachers might have different views about what should be included on the list, for example, some teachers might think that graph paper or calculators should be included, while other teachers might not. These unexpressed differences among the lists would make the resulting data difficult to interpret.

Second, one person could have made an inventory of the entire building. This approach would put a large burden on one person to have enough time to do a thorough job. Also, that person might not know where each teacher keeps manipulatives in a classroom, so it would be easy to overlook some.

Third, teachers could be interviewed about the manipulatives that are available. People's memories are sometimes not complete, so teachers might not remember all of the manipulatives that are available to use. In addition, teachers' responses to questions might not be consistent in terms of each teacher having the same notions of what should be included in a list of manipulatives.

Fourth, students could be questioned about the manipulatives that they use in doing mathematics. These data would be more of a reflection of the use of manipulatives rather than the availability of manipulatives. While both types of information are ultimately useful, the first focus of the committee was on the availability of manipulatives in the building.

Fifth, teachers could keep a log of the manipulatives they use in teaching. Again, these data would reflect use more than availability. This might be a good way to follow up on the initial survey.

Cautions Regarding Misinterpretation

Use of Manipulatives Does Not Guarantee That Students Learn

The recent reforms in mathematics teaching suggested by the National Council of Teachers of Mathematics (NCTM, 1989, 1991) suggest strongly that students need to have manipulatives available to assist them in developing a sophisticated understanding of mathematics concepts. The committee, however, should be careful to point out to teachers that simply having manipulatives in the building is not adequate for guaranteeing that those manipulatives will be used effectively to help students improve in their understanding of important mathematics concepts. It will take several years and more evaluation efforts to know if the workshops that are suggested will actually give teachers information that they can incorporate into their instruction. Even more distant is any verification that changes in instruction will result in improved student performance. That, too, would require extensive evaluation efforts carried out over a period of years after changes in instruction have been implemented. Vignettes that might help structure those evaluation efforts are contained elsewhere in this guide.

4 Vignette Four

Materials for Teaching Statistics

Changes in State Curriculum Guidelines **S**ometimes curriculum changes are dictated by political forces, for example, state legislatures or state school boards of education. In these circumstances, school districts and teachers within those districts have little option but to comply with the decisions and carry them out in the best possible way. It is of course easier to carry out these dictates when teachers believe that the decisions are appropriate, and this is generally the case for the decision to include statistics and probability in the school curriculum. The faculty of Carlton High faced this decision when the state curriculum guide was changed to include a strand on statistics in the Consumer Mathematics course. This change brings the state curriculum guide into better alignment with the *Curriculum and Evaluation Standards* (National Council of Teachers of Mathematics, 1989).

Where, What, and Why?

Built in the late 1970s, Carlton Senior High enrolls 1,250 students in Grades 10 through 12. It draws students from the southern sections of Lake County, an area that is currently experiencing a rapid increase in residential growth. Carlton has a reputation for academic excellence, which serves an important component in the attraction of business and industry. To maintain a semblance of equality among school enrollment figures for the three high schools in the school district, the school board has been forced to redraw district lines twice during the last 5 years.

Carlton's student body comprises primarily upper-income students whose parents are professionally trained or college educated. On the average, about 50% of the graduating senior class each year attend a 4-year college, and about 30% attend a community college or other postsecondary education program. The students at Carlton historically have been a homogeneous group not only economically and educationally but also racially with more than 85% of the students classified as white and not of Hispanic origin. The rapid increase in apartment units in the area, however, is beginning to create a shift in student enrollment patterns; 2 years ago, 9% of the students were minority; last year, 12% were minority; and this year, 14% are minority. Most of the increase is among Asian and Hispanic students, and district officials predict that, within 5 years, about 30% of the students will be from these two groups.

Edwina Fox, principal of Carlton, is proud to be associated with such a fine educational institution. With almost no group tensions among students, Dr. Fox enjoys a friendly, relaxed relationship with both teachers and students. She is proud of the academic and athletic accomplishments of Carlton and is always pleased when Carlton student groups achieve victory over rival schools. With a school staff of 65 teachers, 3 school counselors, 1 school nurse, 1 dropout prevention counselor, 2 media specialists, 3 school secretaries, and 3 assistant principals, Dr. Fox spends the majority of her time working with teachers and staff members to improve the educational effectiveness of Carlton through continuing and focused evaluation. Dr. Fox views her staff as a group of highly trained, professional educators who are experts in their respective fields. In turn, the teachers at Carlton admire and respect Dr. Fox as an educational leader, with the foresight and energy to make Carlton into an educational legend.

Understanding the Problem

Many Teachers Lack Exposure to Statistics Content

The mathematics faculty at Carlton are concerned about their ability to implement the new consumer mathematics curriculum, in part because only two of the seven mathematics teachers ever had a statistics course. Mr. Black, the chairperson of the mathematics department, has decided to call a special faculty meeting to discuss the changes in the consumer mathematics curriculum; prior to the meeting, he circulated copies of the state education department's position paper outlining the need for the additional content along with the expected goals for that content. Because textbooks will not be up for adoption for another 3 years, he knows that the teachers will have to search supplementary resources to find instructional materials to teach the new content.

During the meeting, Ms. Verable, one of the two teachers who had taken a statistics course, expressed concern about whether consumer mathematics students would be able to comprehend the content adequately. "Won't time working on statistics take away from the time those students need just to be able to do the computation that is required on the competency test necessary for graduation?" Two other teachers, however, echoed the philosophy of the state's curriculum guide by commenting that statistics is a very important part of dealing with information in the real world so it is appropriate for the Consumer Mathematics course to give attention to that content. Ms. Preka commented that the state education department had cited the *Curriculum and Evaluation Standards* from the National Council of Teachers of Mathematics (NCTM, 1989) in providing the rationale for inclusion of statistics in Consumer Mathematics courses. "The *Standards* includes a strong statistics standard in the suggested curriculum for Grades 9-12, so the changes we need to implement have a strong national rationale." Discussion of the appropriateness of including statistics in the course continued for about another half hour. Mr. Black decided that it was important for all the teachers to "vent" their views about this topic so that attention could then be directed to the task of planning instruction. At several points in the discussion, Mr. Black, supported by Ms. Preka, reminded the teachers that, because the state education board had decided that statistics must be included, perhaps their more important task should be to find appropriate materials for teaching the content.

Focusing the Evaluation

When the discussion reached a lull, Mr. Black again raised the question, "How should we proceed in identifying appropriate instructional materials for teaching statistics in the Consumer Mathematics course?" The teachers began to brainstorm possible techniques and resources: contact the district's mathematics supervisor as well as other schools to see what they are planning to use in instruction; review high school statistics textbooks and choose chapters that could be used; review catalogs of materials; review the list of publications from the NCTM; review Grades 7 and 8 textbooks; write the state's Department of Education for advice; make up their own materials; contact the local university faculty for advice; and so on.

Identify Clear Instructional Goals   As the brainstorming seemed to lag, Mr. Madson, who had taught consumer mathematics for the past 6 years, suggested that they might want to review the goals for the statistics strand and then develop objectives for instruction before they started looking for instructional materials. "If we know what the purposes of the instruction are, then we ought to be able to select materials that fit our needs better." Ms. Preka supported this notion and asked Mr. Black if the district had developed, or was planning to develop, content objectives for the statistics strand. Mr. Black said that he had contacted the assistant superintendent for curriculum, who said that writing objectives for the statistics strand would probably have to wait until next year. She did suggest, however, that Mr. Black look at the recently published *Evaluating School Programs: An Educator's Guide* and the accompanying *Mathematics Programs: A Guide to Evaluation*, which contained a set of standards and indicators that might prove to be useful.

Mr. Black said that he had obtained a copy of each of these guides and that he had examined the statistics standards from *Mathematics Programs: A Guide to Evaluation*. (See Resource A for the complete list of standards and indicators.) The standards and indicators for statistics are given below.

8. Statistics and Data Analysis
   8.1. Students have opportunities to systematically collect, organize, and describe data.
   8.2. Students have opportunities to construct, read, and interpret tables, charts, graphs.
   8.3. Students have opportunities to formulate and solve problems that involve collecting and analyzing data.
   8.4. Students have opportunities to make inferences and convincing arguments that are based on data analysis and to develop an appreciation for statistical methods as powerful means for decision making.
   8.5. Students have opportunities to understand and apply measures of central tendency, variability, and correlation.

Mr. Madson commented that, except for the last indicator, these indicators could apply to almost any grade level and almost any course that had a statistics strand. Ms. Verable interjected that the indicators were not as specific as she might like, based on her understanding of how to write behavioral objectives. Ms. Preka said that she liked the nonbehavioral nature of these goals, because they allowed teachers quite a lot of flexibility in deciding what instructional activities to use. Mr. Black asked if any of the teachers had serious objections to the way these indicators were worded. After about 15 minutes of discussion, all the teachers agreed that they could accept the indicators and that they felt that they could identify appropriate instructional materials based on these indicators.

Match Materials to Standards and Indicators

Mrs. Hardison, who usually taught tenth-grade geometry, asked how they might translate the indicators into more specific measures that could be applied to the evaluation of instructional materials.

Mr. Madson suggested that it might be appropriate first to decide as a faculty which of the indicators were most important. Then the instructional materials could be matched to these most important indicators.

Mr. Black suggested that the plan outlined by Mr. Madson was a very good one: First determine the most important indicators and then evaluate the available materials using the rank-ordered list of indicators. He asked how they might go about gathering the relevant data on the teachers' rank orderings. Mrs. Hardison said that all they had to do was have each teacher list the indicators in order of importance and then calculate the average rank for each indicator. This would allow all the teachers to have input, but it would not put any teachers on the spot, either by having to explain the reasons for their choices or to vote in front of their peers. All of the teachers thought this approach was appropriate, and they agreed to do it immediately. After the teachers had all ranked the indicators, Mr. Black wrote the ranks on the blackboard and they computed the averages. (See Table 4.1.)

Every teacher selected Indicators 8.1 and 8.2 as the most important for consumer mathematics students, but rankings of the other indicators were not so consistent. In order, the average rankings of the other indicators was 8.5, 8.4, and 8.3; but their averages were similar. From these data, the teachers could see that the evaluation should focus on Indicators 8.1 and 8.2.

How to Evaluate

The next question to be addressed was how the teachers were going to find and evaluate potential supplementary materials for use in consumer mathematics. Mr. Black suggested that they return to the list of sources they had brainstormed earlier: Contact the district's mathematics supervisor as well as other schools to see what they are planning to use in instruction; review high school statistics textbooks and choose chapters that could be used; review catalogs of materials; review the list of publications from the NCTM; review Grades 7 and 8 textbooks; write the state's Department of Education for advice; make up their own materials; contact the local university faculty for advice; and so on.

Most of these suggestions were discounted by the teachers for a variety of reasons. Because all schools in the state were being affected by the changes in the consumer mathematics curriculum, contacting other schools didn't seem to be a very effective choice. High school statistics textbooks might not be written appropriately for consumer mathematics students, though there might be some lesson ideas that could be adapted for use. Using lessons from Grade 7 or 8 textbooks might send the message to students that they simply have to "do again" the same kinds of activities that they had already done before, and, as a

TABLE 4.1   Teacher Rankings

Teacher	Indicator				
	8.1	*8.2*	*8.3*	*8.4*	*8.5*
A	1	2	4	3	5
B	1	2	5	4	3
C	2	1	5	3	4
D	1	2	3	4	5
E	2	1	5	4	3
F	1	2	4	5	3
G	1	2	5	4	3
Average	1.3	1.7	4.4	3.8	3.7

consequence, students might lose interest. The state education department had to remain neutral toward all publishers, so they would likely not be able to recommend any particular set of instructional materials for use. The nearest university was focusing its attention on changes in their teacher preparation programs, so they might be too busy to be able to provide immediate and significant help. Because most of the teachers had not taken a statistics course, they might not have adequate knowledge of the content or appropriate pedagogy to be able to develop their own materials. In addition, this approach would take a considerable investment of time; the teachers were not sure they had enough time available to complete the task.

The remaining two choices (to review catalogs of materials and to review the publication list of the NCTM) seemed like the most promising approaches for finding possible materials to be considered. Mr. Black asked for some volunteers to begin the search process so that examination copies of materials could be ordered. Ms. Preka and Mrs. Hardison agreed to coordinate these efforts. They said that they would get catalogs out of the departmental office and circulate these so that the teachers could mark the materials that seemed most promising. Mr. Black asked Ms. Preka and Mrs. Hardison to be ready to provide an update on this process at the next faculty meeting.

Maintain a Focus on the Evaluation Questions

He then refocused the discussion by asking, "Once we have examination copies in hand, how should we evaluate them?" Ms. Preka suggested that they should focus only on the first two indicators. "Since this will be the first time we have tried to teach statistics to consumer mathematics students, I think we should concentrate our efforts on the two areas that we think are most important. Once we are comfortable teaching those two areas, we can expand the nature of the instruction we provide." Mr. Madson added, "Since most of us haven't even taken a statistics course, we will probably be learning some of the content more or less at the same time as our students, so I would be more comfortable if we kept the instructional materials focused on the most important ideas during the first year." These arguments were quickly agreed on by the remaining teachers, so Mr. Black refocused the discussion on the process of reviewing materials. "What process can we use to be sure that the available supplementary materials get an adequate review?"

Ms. Preka spoke up again. "We're not likely to find a single resource that will completely fill our needs; we'll probably have to pick materials from a variety of sources. So rating each resource holistically might not be the best way. Perhaps we could review materials and identify the best lessons that we might be able to use in consumer mathematics." Mrs. Hardison asked if each teacher would review different materials or if each teacher would review all of the materials they were considering. Mr. Madson suggested that perhaps a blend of these two strategies might be used. "Perhaps two of us should review each supplementary booklet so that there is more than one perspective on each of them. We could then buy multiple copies of the books that seem to have the most materials in them that we want to use. At that point, each of us probably ought to review these few books."

Ms. Verable remarked that, in a recent course she had taken on using computer software to teach mathematics, one of the assignments had been to review software using a form that the instructor had provided. "Could we develop a standard form that we could all use to gather common information on the quality of the materials that we collect?" Mr. Madson asked if they needed to be that formal in their evaluations. "Couldn't we just look at the materials and pick the ones we like best, sort of like the way we ranked the indicators?" The teachers debated these two views for some time before they agreed that it would be better to gather some common information on a common form. But it was clear that the form needed to be flexible, so that teachers would easily be able to express their overall reactions. Because the meeting had gone on for quite some time, Mr. Black asked for another set of volunteers to work on a potential evaluation form. Because of her experience with the software review form, Ms. Verable agreed to work on this. Mr. Madson agreed to help, and the faculty meeting was adjourned.

At the next faculty, Ms. Preka reported that eight different catalogs and the NCTM publications list had been circulated, and that there were four books that had been marked by more than half of the teachers. "Review copies of these books have been ordered."

Formulating Evaluation Criteria

Ms. Verable then reported on the tentative review form that had been developed. "Mr. Madson and I looked at half a dozen software review forms. They all had some sections in common: space to list mathematics objectives, evaluation of the accuracy of the mathematics, effectiveness of feedback to students, methods of instructional delivery (e.g., effective use of sound and visuals), cost (e.g, software and necessary hardware), appropriate grade level(s), supplementary materials needed (e.g., student activity sheets, manipulatives). Obviously, some of these categories would not apply to printed material. We thought, however, that a review form for statistics supplementary materials might need to address some of these same categories, along with some other categories centered on ideas in the *Standards*. We've made copies of our first draft of a form." (See Figure 4.1.)

The teachers spent about 30 minutes discussing the form. In general, they thought it was a good form that had been carefully thought through. They agreed, however, to modify the form to ask specifically about how much of the material relates to statistics and data interpretation and to ask for a description of the "best" activity. In addition, they decided that the inclusion of probability content in the checklist list for content was not really relevant, so those items were removed from the form. The revised form that they all agreed on is shown in Figure 4.2.

Summarizing the Results

The teachers then began the process of evaluating the four books. The sample evaluation form is shown in Figure 4.3, with a summary of the Likert items provided in Table 4.2.

Interpreting the Results

Quantitative Data

The teachers then met to discuss their evaluations. They first began by looking at the summary of the Likert items. They quickly agreed that book D should be eliminated. Although it rated high on the fact that little preparation would be required of teachers, the content of the book seemed somewhat weak in appropriateness and coverage. Similarly, book B did not support experimentation and was not consistent with the *Standards,* so it also was eliminated. The differences between books A and C were much smaller on these items, so the teachers looked at the responses to the open-ended questions on the first page of the evaluation form. (The comments that follow are selected from the teachers' evaluation forms and represent "consensus" opinions.)

Title of Booklet: _____

Publisher: _____ Publication date: _____

Number of pages: _____ Price: _____

What is the main focus of the material?

Is the mathematics correct? If not, explain how it is not accurate.

Is the material at a level that generally seems appropriate for consumer mathematics students? If not, explain how it is inappropriate.

Which of the following topics are covered in the booklet. (Check all that apply.)

____ construction and interpretation of charts, graphs, and so on

____ compute and use measures of center and variability

____ fit curves to data

____ use theoretical and experimental probabilities to solve problems

____ conduct simulations to estimate probabilities

Respond to the following statements, using the following 5-point scale:

1 = Strongly disagree
2 = Somewhat disagree
3 = Uncertain
4 = Somewhat agree
5 = Strongly agree

	Disagree ←→ Agree				
This booklet would be suitable for use in consumer mathematics.	1	2	3	4	5
The coverage of statistics and probability is adequate.	1	2	3	4	5
The materials encourage students to explore and experiment.	1	2	3	4	5
The material is consistent with the mathematics standards and indicators.	1	2	3	4	5
The material is consistent with the NCTM's *Standards.*	1	2	3	4	5
Students would enjoy using the material.	1	2	3	4	5
The materials could be used without extensive preparation.	1	2	3	4	5
Students would not need any prerequisites to use the materials.	1	2	3	4	5
The layout is attractive.	1	2	3	4	5
The material is a good value.	1	2	3	4	5

Figure 4.1. Materials Evaluation Form: First Draft

Title of Booklet: _____

Publisher: _____ Publication date: _____

Number of pages: _____ Price: _____

What is the main focus of the material? (Please list the relevant Indicators.)

About how much of the material is related to statistics and data interpretation?

Are the instructional objectives clear? Are they appropriate for consumer mathematics?

Are assessment materials adequate? If not, do you think it would be difficult to develop assessment materials?

Is the mathematics correct? If not, explain how it is not accurate.

Are the activities designed to facilitate individual work, group work, or both?

Do the materials include suggestions for the use of technology? If so, what technology is needed?

Do the materials require or suggest the use of manipulatives? If so, which ones?

Is the material at a level that generally seems appropriate for consumer mathematics students? If not, explain how it is inappropriate.

Which of the following topics are covered in the booklet. (Check all that apply.)
____ construction and interpretation of charts, graphs, and so on
____ compute and use measures of center and variability
____ fit curves to data

Describe the lesson or activity that seems to you to be most outstanding.

Respond to the following statements, using the following 5-point scale:

> 1 = Strongly disagree
> 2 = Somewhat disagree
> 3 = Uncertain
> 4 = Somewhat agree
> 5 = Strongly agree

	Disagree ◄────► Agree				
This booklet would be suitable for use in consumer mathematics.	1	2	3	4	5
The coverage of statistics and probability is adequate.	1	2	3	4	5
The materials encourage students to explore and experiment.	1	2	3	4	5
The material is consistent with the mathematics standards and indicators.	1	2	3	4	5
The material is consistent with the NCTM's *Standards*.	1	2	3	4	5
Students would enjoy using the material.	1	2	3	4	5
The materials could be used without extensive preparation.	1	2	3	4	5
Students would not need any prerequisites to use the materials.	1	2	3	4	5
The layout is attractive.	1	2	3	4	5
The material is a good value.	1	2	3	4	5

Figure 4.2. Revised Materials Evaluation Form

Title of Booklet: <u>Experiments in the Classroom</u>
Publisher: <u>Grayhouse Publishers</u>　　　　Publication date: <u>1990</u>
Number of pages: <u>85</u>　　　　Price: <u>$12.95</u>
What is the main focus of the material? (Please list the relevant indicators.)
　Students conduct probability experiments (e.g., throw dice) and statistics surveys (e.g., favorite movies, weather data). They then display the data they have gathered and draw conclusions. This addresses both Indicators 8.1 and 8.2.
About how much of the material is related to statistics and data interpretation?
　Most of the material is related. However, I am not sure that the students would find the experiments interesting. Few lessons seem related to consumer mathematics.
Are the instructional objectives clear? Are they appropriate for consumer mathematics?
　The objectives are clear, though they focus too much on probability.
Is the mathematics correct? If not, explain how it is not accurate.
　Yes, it seems correct.
Are the activities designed to facilitate individual work, group work, or both?
　Most of the work can be completed by pairs of students. There is little cooperative work required of students.
Do the materials include suggestions for the use of technology? If so, what technology is needed?
　The only technology suggested is calculators.
Do the materials require or suggest the use of manipulatives? If so, which ones?
　The manipulatives needed are dice and spinners, plus tools to draw graphs (e.g., graph paper, rulers, markers).
Is the material at a level that generally seems appropriate for consumer mathematics students? If not, explain how it is inappropriate.
　It is appropriate, but I am not sure it is interesting.

Which of the following topics are covered in the booklet. (Check all that apply.)
　<u>　x　</u> construction and interpretation of charts, graphs, and so on
　<u>　x　</u> compute and use measures of center and variability
　<u>　　　</u> fit curves to data
Describe the lesson or activity that seems to you to be most outstanding.
　The survey of "students' favorites" (e.g., favorite movies, favorite rock star) seems the most interesting to students. Students might be able to draw conclusions about various subgroups of students (i.e., by gender or grade level).

Respond to the following statements, using the following 5-point scale:
　　　　　1 = Strongly disagree
　　　　　2 = Somewhat disagree
　　　　　3 = Uncertain
　　　　　4 = Somewhat agree
　　　　　5 = Strongly agree

	Disagree ←——→ Agree				
This booklet would be suitable for use in consumer mathematics.	1	2	<u>3</u>	4	5
The coverage of statistics and probability is adequate.	1	2	<u>3</u>	4	5
The materials encourage students to explore and experiment.	1	2	3	<u>4</u>	5
The material is consistent with the mathematics standards and indicators.	1	2	<u>3</u>	4	5
The material is consistent with the NCTM's *Standards*.	1	<u>2</u>	3	4	5
Students would enjoy using the material.	1	<u>2</u>	3	4	5
The materials could be used without extensive preparation.	1	2	3	<u>4</u>	5
Students would not need any prerequisites to use the materials.	1	2	3	<u>4</u>	5
The layout is attractive.	1	2	<u>3</u>	4	5
The material is a good value.	1	<u>2</u>	3	4	5

Figure 4.3. Sample Completed Evaluation Form

TABLE 4.2   Summary of Likert Items

Items	Average for Book			
	A	B	C	D
This booklet would be suitable for use in consumer mathematics.	3.5	4.0	3.5	2.0
The coverage of statistics and probability is adequate.	3.0	3.5	4.0	3.0
The materials encourage students to explore and experiment.	2.5	1.0	3.0	2.5
The material is consistent with the mathematics standards and indicators.	4.0	3.5	4.0	3.0
The material is consistent with the NCTM's *Standards*.	3.0	1.5	2.5	3.0
Students would enjoy using the material.	2.5	3.0	2.5	2.0
The materials could be used without extensive preparation.	3.5	2.5	3.0	3.5
Students would not need any prerequisites to use the materials.	4.5	3.0	3.0	4.0
The layout is attractive.	3.5	3.5	3.5	3.0
The material is a good value.	2.5	3.0	3.0	3.0

Book A had 64 pages and cost $9.95. Its main focus was probability, with only a few activities on statistics. In addition, there were pages on number patterns, mental math, and estimation. About 30% was related to statistics and about 40% was related to probability. There were no obvious mathematics errors in the presentation. The level of the material was generally appropriate, but it was not particularly related to consumer mathematics; the teacher would have to make many of the connections. The variety of statistics topics was not viewed as outstanding, because most of the activities were related to probability. One of the best lessons was a series of games with dice. In one game, students were asked to roll the dice and compute the difference in the two numbers. One player scored a point if the difference was odd, and the other player scored a point if the difference was even. Students had to decide if the game was fair.

Qualitative Data

Book C had 85 pages and cost $12.95. Its main focus was probability experiments and statistics surveys. Students were then asked to display the data they gathered and draw conclusions. Most of the material was related to statistics, even though the data were sometimes generated through probability experiments. Two teachers commented on the "disconnectedness" from real life of much of the material; they felt the probability experiments were sometimes "forced" so that data could be generated. There were no obvious mathematics errors in the presentation. The level of the material was viewed as appropriate but not always interesting to students. The variety of topics was viewed as adequate. One of the most outstanding lessons was a survey of "students' favorites" (e.g., favorite movies, favorite rock stars). One teacher commented that students might be able to identify differences among various subgroups of students (e.g., by gender or grade level) based on the data gathered in the survey and then begin to discuss possible explanations for those differences.

The comments made by the teachers indicated their concern for Indicators 8.1 and 8.2, namely, that students have opportunities both "to systematically collect, organize, and describe data" and "to construct, read, and interpret tables, charts, graphs." After a lengthy discussion, the teachers decided that they needed time for all of them to review these two books in more detail. Mr. Black asked the teachers to review the materials independently and to complete evaluation sheets for both books prior to the next faculty meeting. "I think if we all have completed evaluation sheets at our next meeting, we will be better able to come to some consensus about which book we should use in Consumer Mathematics courses next year."

Two weeks later, the teachers met again to discuss books A and C. Each teacher had reviewed the materials and completed evaluation sheets. Mr. Black asked the teachers to identify the book that they would prefer to use. Opinions split, with four teachers favoring book C and two teachers favoring book A. (Mr. Black did not express his opinion because he was moderating the meeting and was department chair.) The ensuing discussion centered on the ways that the books could be used to address the data objectives for consumer mathematics. The relatively heavy emphasis in book A on probability became fairly clear in the discussion, and the teachers decided to use book C.

Using the Results

Mr. Black agreed to order enough copies of book C for use in consumer mathematics the following year. He then asked the teachers how they should evaluate the effectiveness of their choice. That is, would the materials be useful for helping students learn about statistics?

Plan for Follow-Up to the Evaluation

The teachers discussed this problem for a few minutes, and they agreed that an evaluation plan should have several elements:

1. Gather data at the beginning of each offering of the course on what students know.
2. Gather data at the end of each offering of the course, perhaps for two or three consecutive semesters.
3. Compare the results statistically.

The teachers also agreed that fully developing this plan would take considerable time and effort, because the test that would be used to gather the data would need to be planned very carefully. One of the teachers pointed out, however, that, if they were able to gather these data, they would be well prepared for textbook selection during the next statewide cycle. They would know what kinds of activities were effective with the students, so they would have a good idea of what to look for in new textbooks. Mr. Black also pointed out that they also might be able to share their expertise with other school districts in the state so that all students might benefit from their experiences.

Summary of Evaluation Principles

This example illustrates several important principles that should be kept in mind in all evaluations of school programs.

1. Do not attempt to evaluate every aspect of a program at once. Focus the evaluation by selecting a few indicators of quality. By having each teacher rank the indicators, the two most important indicators surfaced quite clearly. This helped focus the evaluation with a minimum investment of time. The teachers agreed, however, that a thorough evaluation of the effects of using these materials would take much more time and effort.

2. When choosing a method of data collection, try to select an alternative that will minimize the burden on those who will be asked to provide information. Because the teachers themselves were going to evaluate the materials, the development of the evaluation form provided a way that their views could be compared. That is, the data from all the teachers were comparable. The form also helped to focus the attention of each teacher so that the amount of time needed to review any particular set of material was kept to a minimum.

3. Whenever possible, collect information in ways that give every member of the group of interest an opportunity to respond. Because the number of teachers was small, it was both possible and important that all of them be actively involved both in selecting the important indicators to be assessed and in the evaluation of the materials. Gathering information from all teachers would help invest all the teachers in the outcomes so that the adoption of the materials would go as smoothly as possible.

4. Ask questions your information providers are able to answer, and avoid questions that require speculation. In this vignette, each teacher was asked for judgments about the quality of the materials and for a description of the "best" lesson. This allowed teachers to explain their reasoning about their judgments so that other teachers would be able to understand those judgments better.

Alternatives to the Strategy Used Here

There are a number of alternatives that could have been used. First, the teachers could have relied on outside experts (e.g., faculty of the local university) to evaluate the materials. Those people, however, would not be as knowledgeable about the local situation and would not know what materials might best fit the students of Carlton Senior High.

Second, the teachers might have attempted to locate reviews of the books in the professional literature. This would have been time consuming and might have resulted in considerable frustration if the teachers had not been successful at locating any reviews.

Third, the department chairperson could have reviewed the materials using either a personal or a teacher-developed set of criteria and then selected the book to use. This alternative would have effectively prevented constructive input from the teachers who would actually have used the materials in instruction.

Fourth, as part of the initial evaluation, the teachers could have field-tested one or two of the lessons from each book with students in Consumer Mathematics classes. This might have given them a "feel" for the response from students, but, because the materials were so different in their approach to instruction, this procedure might have resulted in inappropriate use of class time, at least in some of the trials.

Cautions Regarding Misinterpretation

The teachers were quite clear that their evaluations were their projections about the potential quality of the materials. As the teachers agreed, there needs to be a separate evaluation of the actual effects of the use of these materials. This evaluation will take considerable effort to design and carry out, and it will require a considerable amount of time, because the materials actually have to be used with students.

Teacher evaluation of materials is only one way to get information about the effectiveness of those materials. Publishers should field-test all materials that they produce for student use, but, because of limitations on development budgets for materials and because of time pressures to meet publication deadlines, many materials are not subjected to these field trials. Teachers need to be alert to the different reactions that students have when new materials are used in instruction for the first time. The concepts that students generalize from instructional materials may not be the ones that the authors of those materials expected to be learned.

5 Vignette Five

Assessing the Effectiveness of Feedback to Students

Feedback on Homework

Part of the reason that students lose interest in mathematics is that they are unsure of their strengths and weaknesses; that is, they lack confidence in knowing how well they can succeed in carrying out mathematical tasks. To help students develop an accurate awareness of those strengths, it is important for teachers to provide regular and accurate feedback to students about their performance. In addition, teachers need to be sure that parents know how well their children are performing so that parents can also support their children in completing mathematics problems. The most regular way for teachers to provide feedback is through their correcting of homework papers. But how do students interpret the comments that teachers make? Do students perceive the messages in the ways that teachers intend?

Where, What, and Why?

South Middle School is a small rural middle school that serves 800 students in Grades 6 through 8. It has a clean, attractive campus that has been well maintained since its construction in the 1950s. Many of South's students live on outlying farms within the county and face an hour's bus ride each morning and afternoon. Of the nonfarm families, a few are blue-collar workers within the county while the remainder find employment in the factories and mills located in surrounding counties. One of three county middle schools, South is the one that remains predominately white racially, with fewer than 10% minority students. While the county is not a high-income area, local school board members have always been able to provide its students with quality education and have been rewarded by well-behaved, interested, and cooperative students and teachers.

Ralph White has been principal of South Middle School for the last 15 years. He is a no-nonsense, strictly business type of administrator, but he clearly loves his school and takes great pride in its accomplishments. The faculty and staff see Mr. White as a true educational leader and typically respond in a positive manner toward his suggestions for improvement.

Helping Students Understand Strengths and Weaknesses

During the past several years, the school counselor has made Mr. White aware of an increasing sense of "drift" among the students about the relevance of mathematics courses for their lives. Although all students understand that they have to take mathematics each year while they are in the middle school, the eighth graders are increasingly expressing an interest in taking general mathematics courses, rather than Algebra I, in high school. The counselor reports that each year she seems to have to talk more and more students into enrolling in Algebra I. When she asked several students why they were not interested in algebra, they typically responded that they didn't "feel comfortable" in mathematics courses and that they were afraid of "being in over their heads." They perceived that mathematics instruction put too much pressure on them, without allowing them adequate information about whether they understood the material. In other courses, in-class projects counted heavily toward their grades and the feedback from teachers and other students seemed to help them develop a sense of "where they stood." But, in mathematics courses, "the teachers seem to keep too much information to themselves" and not let students learn to understand their own strengths and weaknesses.

Outside Observers Can Help Pinpoint Difficulties

Mr. White was concerned about this attitude among students, because he believes that, especially during early adolescence, it is important for students to develop the confidence that they can succeed in all academic areas. The faculty of South Middle School are collectively responsible for the development of the students in the critical 3-year period in early adolescence, so, if students are to develop confidence about their future academic success, it probably has to happen during these years. When Mr. White reported the observations of the counselor to Mrs. Wall, the mathematics department chairperson, she suggested that perhaps she could work with the five mathematics teachers to evaluate how they are currently helping students to develop confidence in doing mathematics and then to consider ways to improve what they are doing. Mr. White suggested that one possible area of consideration might be the ways that the teachers give feedback on a daily basis to students about their performance. He offered to help the teachers in whatever way he could if the teachers decided to evaluate and, of necessity, change the techniques they were currently using.

Evaluations Should Not Be Threatening

As a first step, Mrs. Wall met with the teachers to talk about their perceptions of the observations of the counselor and to decide if there was a problem that needed to be addressed. One teacher was concerned that the sense of Mr. White's comments implied he was seeking a way to expand the existing teacher assessment scheme. She wondered if Mr. White were approaching the situation with the expectation that it was the "failure" of teachers to provide adequate feedback to students. Mrs. Wall was careful to make explicit that at this point she was interested only in whether there was a problem that needed to be addressed. If there were, she said that she would be on her guard to prevent any comparisons of individual teachers. Mrs. Wall stressed that through this evaluation she hoped to discover strengths and weaknesses in the department's instructional program, with the goal of finding ways to improve the learning of students. This seemed to put the teachers at ease so that they could proceed with the discussion.

Focusing the Evaluation

Assess Current Conditions

As an opening question for the discussion, Mrs. Wall asked teachers what kinds of homework and projects they assigned and how they provided information to students on those tasks. Ms. Jackkel, who taught both sixth and seventh grades, started the discussion by saying that she wanted to help students make the transition from elementary school mathematics lessons to middle school lessons, where more and more independent work was required of students. She started the school year in the sixth grade by having students use lots of manipulatives for concept development. By the end of the first semester, she expected those students to be able to figure out more and more of their own errors, so during most of the year she typically marked homework exercises right and wrong and handed those marked papers back to students. In the seventh grade, she often had students mark each other's homework papers as she read the answers out of the teachers guide. All of the other four teachers supported this general philosophy, with two of them commenting that this was the way that they had learned mathematics, and therefore they thought it was the most appropriate way to teach mathematics.

Mrs. Wall then asked what the students did when homework papers were returned. Mr. Klimer said that his eighth-grade students usually just put the papers in their notebooks without looking at them. Ms. Graber agreed that her sixth-grade students also just put the papers away without looking at them. She said that she had never really thought about how the students interpreted the grades on homework, but until this minute she assumed that students used the corrected papers for studying when they got home. Simply raising the question of what students did with their papers had caused her to think about whether they understood the mistakes they had made. "Are there some standard techniques for helping students make sense of their corrected homework papers?" Mr. Prokosch, who taught seventh and eighth grades, then asked if their "laissez-faire" handling of homework grading was the best way to serve the students at South. "Maybe there are better ways for us to be grading homework."

Mrs. Mason, who taught eighth-grade mathematics and science, raised the issue that they probably didn't know what the students thought about the corrections of their homework papers. "We shouldn't make wholesale changes in what we are doing just because we think there might be a problem. Maybe we ought to find out how students are dealing with the information we give them on corrected papers and then try some small experiments to see if there are better ways."

Mrs. Wall commented that the *Professional Standards for Teaching Mathematics* (National Council of Teachers of Mathematics, 1991) suggested that more and more cooperative work, rather than individual work, seemed to be the "wave of the future" in mathematics teaching. Developing teamwork skills seems to be something that businesses want and need, so students probably need opportunities to work together as they internalize understanding of a problem or its solution. "Perhaps there are ways that we might be able to incorporate more group work in the kinds of homework assignments that we ask students to carry out. I wonder if doing this would cause us to change the ways we provide feedback to students."

Seeking Help From Professional Resources

Ms. Graber said that she had recently been to a regional conference where one of the speakers talked about alternative assessment ideas, including evaluation of cooperative group work, portfolios, classroom observations coupled with individual interviews of students, and holistic scoring of problem solving. The speaker had referenced a new series on evaluation of school programs, which included *Evaluating School Programs: An Educator's Guide* and *Mathematics Programs: A Guide to Evaluation*. "The approach taken in these books seems to be quite consistent with that proposed by the NCTM in its *Standards*. Because both books were available for purchase in the exhibits area, I bought them and have them with me today. Perhaps they would be useful to us, since there are a number of standards on assessment." Ms. Graber turned to Resource A and looked at the assessment standards, especially those related to the way that feedback is given to students. The most relevant indicators are presented below:

16. Mathematical Power
    16.1. Students know and can use mathematics concepts, procedures, and problem-solving strategies appropriate to a given situation.
    16.2. Students have opportunities to develop an appreciation for the use of mathematics in a variety of real-world settings.

17. Mathematical Disposition
    17.1. Student assessments measure confidence in, and perseverance for, using mathematics to solve problems, to communicate ideas, and to reason.
    17.2. Student assessments measure flexibility, interest, curiosity, and inventiveness in exploring mathematical ideas and trying alternative methods in solving problems.
    17.3. Student assessments measure inclination to monitor and reflect on their own thinking and performance.
    17.6. Counselors and mathematics teachers maintain effective communication for advising students about program decisions and for planning of instructional schedules.

18. Alignment
    18.3. Teaching practices include use of different grouping strategies (i.e., large group, small group, individual) and appropriate manipulatives and technologies.
    18.4. Instruction is adapted in terms of pacing and learning styles to match the students and the content.

20. Appropriate Assessment Methods and Uses
    20.2. Appropriate diagnostic measures and tools are available to assess student needs and are used for prescribing appropriate instructional activities for individual students.
    20.3. Teachers use acceptable methods for recording students' progress.
    20.4. Teachers provide consistent evaluation and interpretation of student progress.
    20.5. Communication of student progress to students and parents is effective.

Mrs. Wall commented that these indicators suggest that students need to have access to a wide variety of information about their progress toward understanding the important mathematical ideas and processes. Simply giving students information about right/wrong would not seem to be adequate for helping students attain all the goals implicit in these standards. Mrs. Mason agreed that these standards and indicators put a great deal of responsibility on teachers to be sure that students understand what their level of understanding is at any given time. "Perhaps we do need to rethink the types of feedback we give to students as well as try to determine what messages students get from the feedback we give."

Collecting Information

Clarify the Question

Mrs. Wall then posed the question of how they could find out how the "average" student interpreted the information given under current practices. Mr. Prokosch suggested that they could survey students to find out the answer. Ms. Jackkel asked how many students they would have to survey and whether a survey of middle school students would yield information that was believable. "How do we ask questions that will accurately reveal what middle school students know?"

Mr. Klimer suggested that it might be more profitable for the teachers to work with small groups of students and different ways of giving feedback and to observe carefully how they dealt with the different ways of providing that feedback. Mrs. Mason agreed that middle school students might not be able to respond well to interview questions and that observing students might be a more satisfactory way to get the information they needed about the effects of different ways of providing feedback to students.

Alternative Feedback Techniques

Ms. Graber, however, intervened at this point to raise the question of what ways they might identify for giving feedback to students. Mrs. Wall agreed that the discussion had "gotten a bit ahead of itself" in the sense that the teachers had not adequately discussed alternatives for providing feedback to students. Attention, then, turned to that important question. The teachers began to brainstorm and came up with a variety of suggestions: Write general comments on homework about the overall quality of the work; circle the first incorrect step in each solution; provide the correct solution to each problem in writing; suggest how the ideas in a solution should be reorganized; discuss sample (and frequent) incorrect solutions in class without identifying which students actually attempted each incorrect solution; and so on. Ms. Graber suggested that it might be important to know what students were currently doing with the limited kinds of feedback being provided. She further suggested that it might be necessary to talk to a few students to determine if they regularly made any use of this information. "For example, if I simply tell students whether their solutions are right or wrong, could they find the errors in their solutions?" Mrs. Wall said that she was intrigued with that idea; could students find their own errors if they were told which problems contained errors? "Maybe we could return a marked homework assignment and ask students to write down the errors that they think they made on each problem that is incorrect. Then we could try out some different techniques for giving feedback and reassess the success that students have in identifying their errors." Mr. Prokosch, Ms. Jackkel, and Mrs. Mason immediately picked up on this idea as very appropriate, but Mrs. Mason responded, "Let's consider how this idea would work in class. We could return a homework assignment with the problems scored as right/wrong and ask students to write down the error that they think they made for each problem they got wrong. Then, after we worked with students using several different techniques, we could choose another homework assignment and ask students again to identify the errors they made on each of the incorrect problems. But what are the interventions that we might use?"

Mr. Klimer suggested that it would be simplest just to give students rich feedback about anything the teachers thought was relevant for the solution of the problems. Ms. Graber interjected that she had recently taken a mathematics education research course, and she was certain that there was a body of research about the use of comments on homework. She volunteered to try to locate some of that literature and to report back to the teachers about what she found. Ms. Jackkel suggested that they might want to work with small groups of students in their classes so that they could try out a variety of different techniques.

Understanding How Students Use a Teacher's Feedback

Mrs. Wall brought the group back to an overlooked point: How do we measure the students' use of the feedback we provide? Mr. Klimer suggested that they might simply compute the percentage of incorrectly worked problems for which students could identify the incorrect step in the attempted solution. Then, after different techniques were tried, the corresponding percentages could be calculated. If the percentages increased, then one could conclude that the interventions were more successful than the current techniques for providing feedback.

The teachers spent about 45 minutes in discussion of whether this process would provide them the information they were seeking. The major concern addressed was whether improvements in identifying errors might simply reflect increased skill that could be attributed to practice. Most of the teachers agreed that students were unlikely to "spontaneously" improve at identification of the error in an incorrectly worked problem. Rather, if there were improvements, they would most likely be due to the effects of different kinds of activities conducted in class. At the conclusion of this discussion, the teachers agreed that the process suggested by Mr. Klimer seemed quite likely to generate information directly relevant to the problem of students' use of feedback to improve their knowledge. Mrs. Mason commented again that her "sense of the standards and indicators" was that students needed to be reflective about their own strengths and weaknesses. "I think the kind of information that we are talking about getting from students will help them understand themselves better, but it will also help us understand how we can make instruction more appropriate to our students' needs." Mrs. Wall pointed to Indicators 17.3, 20.2, and even 18.3, to some extent, as the indicators that seemed to match Mrs. Mason's observations.

A Plan for Gathering Data

Discussion then turned to setting a schedule for carrying out this process. First, the teachers agreed that they needed to gather baseline data about how well students could identify errors in incorrectly worked problems. The plan they adopted was to take the next three homework assignments, score those assignments as right/wrong, return the papers to students, and ask students to identify the first major error in each of the problems marked incorrect. Each paper would be scored according to the percentage of "explanations" that the students could provide for the incorrectly worked problems. Then they would try out interventions with small groups of students and repeat the process for three more homework assignments. For each set of three assignments, the average percentage would be the data that would be compared.

But what interventions would be tried? The teachers decided that they needed time to think about these, so the discussion was postponed until the next departmental meeting. Mrs. Wall asked the teachers to try to read some of the literature on homework to get some ideas for what interventions might be appropriate. Ms. Graber agreed that she would try to be prepared to lead a discussion on this topic.

At the next meeting, Ms. Graber led the discussion, which included brainstorming a variety of ideas. Many of these ideas had been suggested earlier: circling the first major error, listing the major mathematics ideas that might have been used to solve the problem, working problems using different problem-solving strategies, having students find errors in problems that were intentionally incorrectly worked by the teacher, and so on. The teachers decided that they would try three different interventions, as described below.

Comparing Three Different Feedback Techniques

(1) Circle the first major error. Each teacher would circle the step in the solution that contained the first major error, without indicating precisely what the error was. For example, in the following problem, the second partial product would be circled, because that is the first indication of a major misunderstanding of a mathematics concept (i.e, place value). The arithmetic error in the first step would not be circled, because that may have been only a careless mistake (e.g., thinking 15 instead of 16 and writing the 5).

$$\begin{array}{r} 5.2 \\ \times\ \underline{1.8} \\ 415 \\ \underline{52\ \ } \\ 4.67 \end{array}$$

(2) Provide feedback holistically on attempted solutions. Teachers would score problems holistically, for example, on a 4-point scale. A score of 4 indicates that the problem was solved correctly and that a clear explanation was given for the major steps in the solution. A score of 3 indicates that the problem was solved correctly but that adequate explanation was not given. A score of 2 indicates that the solution process was generally correct but that some error was made that prevented the correct solution from being obtained. A score of 1 indicates that the solution process was not correct and probably would not lead to the correct solution. A score of 0 indicates that the problem was not attempted or that the student's efforts could not be understood. This scoring scheme does not require detailed reading of each step in a solution. Instead, the teacher has to view the solution as a whole and make a judgment about the overall quality of that solution. Most teachers report that, after a little practice, holistic scoring schemes are relatively easy to use and the feedback seems to be consistent across students.

(3) Give correct answers to incorrectly worked problems, with students reworking those problems. Teachers simply mark each incorrectly worked problem and write the answer next to the attempted solution. Students then are expected to rework those problems for homework.

Implementing the Interventions

Mr. Prokasch asked if all of these interventions had to be implemented at the same time. Ms. Graber said that her review of the homework literature had indicated that different strategies for assigning and grading homework seemed to have differential effects, so each teacher might have to split a class into thirds, with each third getting one of the different interventions. Mr. Klimer suggested that an alternate strategy would be to implement each of the interventions one at a time, with students asked to explain their incorrect homework problems after each intervention. Mr. Prokosch said that, in a research methods course he took as part of his master's degree program, he had learned that there might be some bias in results if all of the interventions were conducted in the same order, so he suggested that, if this alternative were used, the teachers might have to write the three interventions on slips of paper and choose the order of the interventions at random by drawing the slips out of an envelope. Several of the other teachers agreed that they needed to avoid bias in order of implementation of the interventions, and the "random draw" process seemed like an easy way to do this. Ms. Jackkel then asked how long each intervention would last. Mrs. Mason suggested that a week for each might be about right, because it would give students a chance to get used to the new types of feedback. Ms. Graber, however, was not sure that a week was long enough. Mrs. Wall pointed out, however, that they didn't have a lot of time to experiment, given all of the other responsibilities that they had to fulfill. "If there are not differences among the interventions in one week each, then we might have to consider lengthening the time devoted to implementing each intervention."

But the question remained about which style of intervention to use. Mrs. Wall spoke in favor of the first strategy, namely, having all three interventions used in a class at once, though with different groups of students. "I know that it may seem to be difficult to manage, but this plan would seem to provide information more quickly, and it would avoid the problem of having students interpret their errors too frequently. I would be suspicious that, if we asked them to interpret their errors four different times in a month, we might simply be measuring the improvement in their skills at interpreting errors." After a brief discussion, a majority of teachers agreed with this position, so their attention turned to planning the schedule for studying the effects of the interventions. Because the three interventions would occur simultaneously, the teachers agreed to let their experiment run for 2 weeks.

The teachers spent another of their departmental meetings discussing the nature of the interventions. The first question was related to splitting up each class into thirds. Most of the teachers had had some experience in a statistics course using a random number table, but they needed time to refresh their skills. Mr. Prokosch had completed his research course most recently, so the majority of this explaining fell on him. Through an example, he explained how a class could be randomly split into thirds. First, by using the class roster, each student was assigned a number. Then two-digit numbers were read from the random number table until one third of the students' numbers had been written down. This group would receive the first intervention. Then the next third of the students' numbers were written down by reading two-digit numbers from the random number table. These students would receive the second intervention. The remaining students would receive the third intervention.

Next, the teachers had to deal with development of a common understanding of each intervention. Circling the first major error meant that each problem would have to be read fairly carefully to determine where each student had made the first major incorrect move. Holistic scoring was somewhat more problematic in terms of reaching a common understanding. Fortunately, the NCTM has published a short guide to various techniques for scoring problem solving (Charles, Lester, & O'Daffer, 1987), and Mrs. Wall had a copy in the department office. So the teachers were able to read the explanations in that booklet and to reach consensus by practicing on the examples of student

TABLE 5.1   Baseline Results: Students' Explanations of Errors

Teacher	Average Percentage of Errors Explained
A	27
B	22
C	34
D	16
E	20
F	19

work contained in that source. Giving positive feedback for attempting a solution was easy to reach consensus on; all of the teachers were philosophically attuned to this technique, because the philosophy of the school was consistent with this approach.

Organizing and Analyzing the Data

Organizing the Baseline Data

The first step was to get some baseline data by asking students to explain their errors on three successive homework assignments. It wasn't a surprise that students initially had a difficult time doing this. The average percentages for the teachers are shown in Table 5.1.

In the 2 weeks after the initial cycle of asking students to explain their errors, each of the teachers divided one class in thirds and provided each third with one of the interventions for feedback on homework. During the following week, the teachers again asked students to explain their errors on three successive homework assignments. The results are shown in Table 5.2.

In all of the classes, the first intervention seemed to have the most effect on students' abilities to explain their errors. The effects of the other two interventions were mixed; in some classes, holistic scoring seemed better, while, in other classes, the correct answer with reworking of the incorrectly worked problems seemed better.

Interpreting the Results

Major Conclusions

The major conclusion of these data seems to be that circling the first major error in a problem seems to help students to learn to be better able to explain their errors. Upon reflection, the teachers thought these results were reasonable. By circling the first major error, the teachers had been able to focus the attention of the students on one of the critical mistakes in the problem. Of course, it was still up to the students to take advantage of that information by internally monitoring their work so that they did not continue to make the same error. The other two methods of providing feedback to students may not have

TABLE 5.2   Percentage of Errors Explained by Students After Interventions

Intervention	Teacher					
	A	B	C	D	E	F
Circling first error	47	53	63	38	52	58
Holistic scoring	38	49	49	33	46	47
Correct answer with reworking	35	50	49	35	44	49

provided information specific enough that students could change their approaches to solving problems. It is possible, however, that, as students become more sophisticated in their self-monitoring processes (e.g., in their metacognitive processing), one of the other types of feedback might become more useful in improving performance.

Using the Results

Follow-Up May Need to Be Long Term

At the next departmental meeting, which Mr. White attended, Mrs. Wall reviewed the results of the evaluation and then asked the teachers what they thought they should do next. "How can we use this information to improve feedback to students? Is there any other information that we might want to know?" Mr. Klimer suggested that they might want to talk to a few students from each group to see how the students tried to make use of the information provided by each intervention. "But I don't know if we have enough time to carry this out." Ms. Graber agreed that simply looking at the one measure of student performance might not be enough. "We really need to find out what students are thinking so that we have a more complete picture of the effects of our feedback."

The teachers agreed that they might have become somewhat too comfortable with their previous instructional techniques (e.g., simply marking homework as right/wrong) and that this evaluation exercise had opened their eyes to the fact that teaching and learning were far more complex than they had imagined. Ms. Graber said, "I never knew quite how influential different forms of feedback could be in increasing students' understanding of their own work. I thought that simply assigning homework and making sure that students did the homework was about all that I needed to do. Now I see that I have to be more careful in structuring the information that I give to students about their work." To evaluate teaching without looking at the effects of feedback on learning is to look only at a small piece of the total picture. This mathematics faculty had become so excited about the possibilities of increasing learning through thoughtful program evaluation that they agreed that they needed to expand their use of program evaluation techniques.

Mr. White was equally impressed with the evaluation efforts by the teachers, and he asked Mrs. Wall to make a presentation to the total faculty and to the PTA. "Perhaps there are other departments that have concerns about some aspect of their instructional program but don't know how to adequately address those concerns. The model provided by the mathematics department faculty may help others begin their own evaluation effort. I would also like parents to see an example of the type of professional activity our teachers are involved in."

Summary of Evaluation Principles

This example illustrates several important principles that should be kept in mind during all evaluations of school programs.

1. Do not attempt to evaluate every aspect of the program at once. Focus the evaluation on a few indicators. The teachers began with a concern about students' knowledge of personal skills in carrying out mathematics tasks. Through a series of discussions centered on Mr. White's concern about feedback to students, the evaluation focused on how various types of feedback might effect students' skill at explaining errors. Other possible avenues for evaluation (e.g., students' knowledge of relevant mathematics concepts) remain open for investigation.

2. Minimize the burden on those who will provide the information. The data were gathered as part of regular homework assignments that teachers would have given even if the evaluation had not been carried out. The teachers had to reach agreement about the nature of the interventions, and they had to spend the time necessary to implement the interventions by providing feedback specific to each intervention, but the burden on the teachers was minimal. In addition, gathering the data required minimal class time, and so it created minimal interruption to regular instruction.

3. Try to collect information from all members of the group of interest. All students from the classes involved participated by explaining their errors. Sampling students from each class would have reduced the amount of data gathered, but implementing the interventions with only some of the students in each class might have been more difficult to manage for the teachers.

4. Try to verify information by asking more than one question about each important issue or dimension of the problem. Asking students to explain their errors on three successive homework assignments helped to make the data more reliable. Students who worked all of the problems on an assignment would not have much opportunity to explain errors, simply because errors didn't occur. Averaging across three assignments gave each student more chances to be in a position of being able to explain errors. This helped students demonstrate clearly what they could do.

Alternatives to the Strategy Used Here

Drawbacks of Interviewing Students

There are other ways that relevant data could have been gathered. For example, students could have been interviewed, but this process would have taken considerable time and would have been subject to the need to make the teachers all equally good at interviewing. Allowing teachers to evaluate students' explanations away from the pressures of the classroom made the tasks of evaluating students' explanations and computing the percentages easier.

Alternatively, teachers could have constructed a "test" in which there were fictitious solutions to problems that contain predetermined errors. Students could then have been tested by asking them to find the error embedded in each such solution. This would require the students to figure out the intended error, however, and would have made the task of explaining the errors less authentic. By asking students to explain their own errors, the students were likely to be more engaged in the task and to give better responses.

Cautions Regarding Misinterpretations

Need for Multiple Sources of Information

Based on the results of this evaluation, it would be very easy to conclude that all teachers should begin to circle the first major error in each attempted solution to each problem on homework. Ms. Graber's suggestion that the teachers needed to find out more about what the students were thinking about, however, is a critical concern. One measure cannot tell the whole story. Multiple sources of information are needed if teachers are to get a true picture of the effects of their feedback on students' learning. Evaluation is a long-term affair.

The evaluation did point out that the type of feedback is critical to improving students' learning. Marking papers is only one way to provide feedback, however. Students need to become skilled at providing feedback to themselves. After all, one of the goals of schooling is to help students become self-reliant rather than teacher reliant. Asking students to interpret feedback (e.g., by explaining why the circled step in a solution is wrong) helps teachers monitor the metacognitive skills of students. When deficiencies are noted, the teacher can help students work on developing the necessary skills.

Feedback During Instruction

Teachers should also consider how feedback about students' problem-solving skills might be given during instruction, without waiting for homework papers to be collected and marked. For example, students could provide feedback to each other or could maintain a mathematics journal in which they individually reflect on their problem-solving skills. These techniques might also have a payoff in helping students become more confident in their abilities to learn on their own, without waiting for directions from teachers. Assuming personal responsibility for learning would seem to be important for keeping students engaged in mathematics learning throughout their lives.

6

Vignette Six

Planning for Professional Growth

The publication of the *Professional Standards for Teaching Mathematics* (National Council of Teachers of Mathematics, 1991) has been instrumental in helping teachers begin to rethink the opportunities and the responsibilities that they have in enhancing their own understanding of mathematics and mathematics teaching. The recent concerns expressed in the many national reports issued about mathematics and science education have helped to stimulate development of many new initiatives for inservice programs for mathematics teachers at all levels. Teachers thus have unprecedented opportunities to engage in professional development.

Where, What, and Why?

Evaluations Should Respond to Community Needs

River Bend Elementary School is located in a remote rural area of Johnson County. Built in the late 1960s, it has a student body of about 250 students in Grades 1 through 6. River Bend draws students from all sections of the county, an area primarily supported by farming, light manufacturing, and jobs in the service industry. Because so few jobs are available within the county, most residents seek employment elsewhere, thus creating a tremendous drain upon the working population of Johnson County. As a result, the local chamber of commerce finds it difficult to attract new business and industry to an area already in the midst of an economic slump. About 45% of the students at River Bend are black, and about 55% are white.

Program Changes Need Supportive Environments

River Bend Elementary School has often been described as a school in trouble. With almost no leadership and poor discipline, River Bend became a school that could not attract quality teachers, that was typically ranked at the bottom of the county's test scores, and where racial tensions among parents were becoming more intense. The school board decided to move Philip James into the principalship of River Bend. Mr. James had been a principal for 7 years, and he had gained the respect of many people in the district for his willingness to experiment with new ideas and his willingness to support teachers who wanted to experiment with new instructional techniques.

Discrepancy Analysis

When Mr. James was in his second year as principal of River Bend, he attended a statewide meeting of elementary school principals where he learned of a statewide project, funded by a U.S. Department of Education grant to the major state university, that was designed to improve elementary school mathematics instruction. The overall plan was to help "lead teachers" become more expert in mathematics instruction and support those lead teachers as they worked with colleagues in the local school buildings. In this project, two lead teachers are identified for each building. Then, all the teachers in a building are asked to complete a needs assessment form that asked for perceptions about both the importance of particular aspects of mathematics instruction and the degree to which those aspects were currently being achieved. The difference between the importance and achievement of a topic was called the "discrepancy" for that topic. If a topic was viewed as highly important but not very well achieved, that is, if the discrepancy was high, then inservice on that topic would seem to be required as part of an attempt to improve mathematics instruction. The needs assessment information was collated and returned to the teachers. The lead teachers worked with the faculty and the principal to create a school improvement plan for mathematics instruction; this plan was sent to the project director. Once the school improvement plans from all the project schools were collected by the project director, she planned a summer workshop for the lead teachers that was designed to respond to the needs most often identified in those school improvement plans. These lead teachers returned to the school during the following school year to conduct workshops for the other teachers in their buildings. This way, all of the teachers got access to some of the information from the summer workshop.

Because this project was federally funded, the project director had decided to keep the forms in the public domain so that other people

Goals of Instruction

1. Mathematics is presented as a subject to be explored through "what if" situations rather than as a series of facts and algorithms to be memorized.
2. The mathematics curriculum presents a balanced treatment of all of the strands of the state framework.

Mathematics Content

3. Students explore geometric figures and develop spatial sense.
4. Problem solving is emphasized; students formulate and solve their own problems using a variety of strategies and materials.
5. Students are encouraged to communicate about mathematical ideas through reading, writing, and active discussion.

Teaching Practices

6. Teachers act as facilitators rather than transmitters of knowledge; mathematical ideas are explored with students rather than presented to students.
7. Teachers provide learning tasks that are problematic, that have nonobvious solutions, and that promote "what if" explorations by students and teachers.

Figure 6.1. Sample Items From the Needs Assessment

could use them, so Mr. James had picked up copies of the needs assessment forms at the end of the session he had attended. (Samples of the items are presented in Figure 6.1.) The items were grouped into three main categories: goals of instruction, mathematics content, and teaching practices.

Successful Ideas Can Be Modified for Local Use

Although it was too late to participate in the project, Mr. James thought that it might be possible for his 12 teachers to carry out the needs assessment process and development of a school improvement plan. They could then schedule their own schoolwide inservice in support of this plan. So he decided to take the idea back to the next faculty meeting and see if the teachers would be interested in trying it out.

Focusing the Evaluation

Relating Teacher Development to Program Needs

When Mr. James distributed the reminder letter for the next faculty meeting, he reminded the teachers that last year he had given them each a copy of *Mathematics Programs: A Guide to Evaluation,* and he asked them to bring their copies to the meeting. At the meeting, Mr. James described the project he had heard about and distributed copies of the needs assessment forms he had obtained at the principals' conference. "From my perspective, this seems like it might be important for helping us decide where we should focus efforts for our own professional development. That is, what is it about our current program that we think is most important but that we are achieving least? A professional development program ought to help us decrease that discrepancy." Mr. James reminded the faculty that last year they had discussed *Mathematics Programs* and *Evaluating School Programs: An Educator's Guide* that recently had been published. "The standards and indicators section of *Mathematics Programs* lists some things that might help us focus our professional development efforts. I hope that whatever we do about conducting a needs assessment will have some impact on our professional development plans." He called their attention to Standard 15 (in Resource A) in *Mathematics Programs*.

15. Teacher Enhancement

    15.1. Teachers of mathematics participate in ongoing mathematics inservice programs, college-level programs, institutes, and conferences.

    15.2. Provisions are made for teachers to meet with each other to share concerns, confer about individual students, and plan mathematics and interdisciplinary programs.

    15.3. Publications and materials from professional mathematics organizations are available in the school, and a mathematics resource area is available to teachers.

    15.4. The principal provides instructional leadership and support for the mathematics program.

    15.5. Mathematics teachers have input into the planning of new or renovated facilities.

    15.6. Teachers have input into selection of textbooks, supplemental materials for the classroom, and materials collections in libraries or media centers.

Ms. Ward, a fourth-grade teacher, commented that she had not thought much about the difference between the importance of an outcome and the degree to which that outcome was being achieved. "Won't our perceptions of these two aspects be similar? After all, won't we spend most of our instructional time on what we think is important?" Ms. Guthrie, a second-grade teacher, commented that she felt that in general she would agree with that view. "But, for example, I think that it is important for children to be able to discuss their mathematical ideas. Yet, I don't feel like I am able to accomplish that goal very well. 'Developing discussion skills' is an area that I would rank high in importance but lower in achievement, at least in my classroom." Two other teachers were then able to offer other examples of areas of mathematics instruction that they had recently come to feel were important but that they did not feel they were achieving well.

Professional Organization Publications Can Help in Evaluation Efforts

Mrs. Edwards then said that, when she attended the state mathematics conference the previous year, she had attended a session on program evaluation. "This sounds somewhat like what I remember hearing at that time. The NCTM publications booth had a booklet on program evaluation that I bought. My recollection is that it is similar to what we are talking about here. Let me go get it from my closet and let's look at that too." In a few minutes, she returned with a copy of *A Guide for Reviewing School Mathematics Programs* (Blume & Nicely, 1991). Mrs. Edwards opened that book and began to examine it with Mr. Samuelson, a first-grade teacher. They found that the forms contained in the booklet were similarly structured; teachers were asked to rank the importance and the achievement of various goals of the mathematics program. The booklet, however, contained forms that dealt with aspects of the curriculum that were not covered on the forms Mr. James had given them, for example, teachers and school administration.

Mr. Samuelson suggested that a "show of hands" be taken to see if the teachers supported the idea presented by Mr. James. "I personally think it would be interesting to find out if there are areas of the mathematics program that we can agree are important but not well achieved." Mr. James asked if there were any objections to taking a vote. As there were none, he asked how many teachers would be interested in completing some form of the needs assessment and then planning an inservice program around those needs. Nine of the teachers voted in favor, and three said that they weren't sure.

How to Evaluate

Mr. James asked for volunteers to plan and carry out the needs assessment. Mr. Samuelson, Mrs. Edwards, and Ms. Guthrie raised their hands. Ms. Guthrie suggested that, because Mrs. Edwards had some familiarity with the forms in the NCTM book, she should chair the team. Mrs. Edwards agreed that she was willing to do this, so Mr. James asked the team to come to the next faculty meeting with some suggestions for how to proceed.

Comparing Evaluation Tools Helps Focus the Evaluation

The next afternoon, the three teachers met to consider how best to proceed. Ms. Guthrie suggested that they compare the forms Mr. James had given them with those in the NCTM book on evaluating programs. The project forms had three categories (goals of instruction, mathematics content, and teaching practices) while the NCTM book had six categories (goals, curriculum, instruction, evaluation, teachers, and administration), with the curriculum category divided into three parts (K-4, 5-8, and 9-12). Mr. Samuelson said that, if their goal was to improve the instructional program, then perhaps they should focus on the curriculum section of the NCTM book. Mrs. Edwards and Ms. Guthrie agreed, so they turned to that section of the book and began to examine the items.

The first problem they encountered was that the items were grouped by grade levels K-4 and 5-8, whereas the grades in River Bend Elementary School were 1 to 6. Ms. Guthrie suggested that they could give the appropriate forms to the appropriate teachers, but upon reflection she realized that this would make the synthesis of the data difficult. "Since there are only 12 teachers, we would have one set of data from eight teachers in Grades 1-4 and data from four teachers in Grades 5-6. It might be difficult for us to agree on what aspects of our program are most important for inclusion in the school improvement plan." Mrs. Edwards suggested that they might be able to "pick and choose" from among the items and create their own needs assessment form. None of the teachers could see any serious problem with this approach, so they decided to examine the items from both K-4 and 5-8 to identify the items they wanted to include.

Refocusing of the Evaluation Can Occur at Any Time

They began by examining the items dealing with numeration and computation, because they felt that those areas constituted the major part of the instructional program at River Bend. As they read through the items, they began to feel somewhat uncomfortable, because the items seemed to be written with an image of mathematics instruction that wasn't quite consonant with the program at River Bend. For example, in the K-4 category, one of the items dealt with operational sense and another item dealt with use of a variety of algorithms. Mr. Samuelson commented that he thought there was only one addition algorithm. "What do you think is meant by a variety of algorithms?" Their concerns prompted them to look at other content areas to see if there were similar difficulties with the focus of River Bend's program as compared with the items in the forms. The teachers noticed that there was a heavy emphasis on manipulatives and technology in all of the areas. Mrs. Edwards commented that she wasn't sure if their program was close enough to the vision represented by the NCTM forms for those forms to be useful as a needs assessment. "If the mismatch between our program and the vision of the items we use is too great, we might not generate any information that is useful to us. Maybe we need to step back a little and decide if we can move directly to an evaluation of our program. Perhaps we need to do a needs assessment on the goals and objectives of our program as a first step."

The teachers reflected on this comment for several minutes before anyone spoke again. Then Ms. Guthrie suggested that, if their program wasn't headed in the same direction as the current reform movements in mathematics education, it would probably be very reasonable to examine their goals. "We may need to redirect what we are doing and the ways we are doing those things as a first step toward revamping our program." Mrs. Edwards and Mr. Samuelson agreed that the curriculum items were problematic and that they needed to approach the needs assessment task a little differently. The focus on goals and instructional techniques seemed appropriate, so they began to examine those items in the NCTM book.

Again, the teachers were almost immediately uncomfortable. Mr. Samuelson commented that the items on goals were awfully general and that the items on instruction were all too broad and too generic. For example, one goal statement talked about helping students "develop their full potential in mathematics," and one instruction item dealt with the use of "varied instructional strategies." "None of the instructional items seem to be related to any specific content or grade level, and the goal statements are so general that everyone would have to agree that they are important." Ms. Guthrie suggested that they review the items in the same two categories from the form that Mr. James distributed at the previous faculty meeting. The sense of the teachers was that these items were better, but they were still somewhat general. Ms. Guthrie speculated that perhaps the NCTM document was more general because it had to deal with K-12 mathematics programs for the entire country. "The forms Mr. James gave us were developed for elementary schools in this state, so the project could focus better on the aspects of elementary school mathematics that would be important for schools like ours."

Evaluation of Fundamental Questions Is Important

The teachers' discussion returned to the problem of how to proceed. They reaffirmed their consensus that jumping into an evaluation of the content of the River Bend mathematics program would be premature. Rather, they felt that a focus on more basic questions was needed. After a lengthy dialogue, they decided that the items related to goals and teaching techniques from the needs assessment form distributed by Mr. James would be the best items to use. Mrs. Edwards agreed to present these plans at the next faculty meeting.

At that meeting, Mr. James asked Mrs. Edwards to provide an update on the progress of the three teachers. She presented their suggestions. "The items on curriculum seem to assume that the mathematics program is in step with the current reform movement in mathematics education. Before we evaluate our curriculum, the three of us feel that it is important to know how much agreement the faculty have on the vision of the mathematics program at River Bend as well as on the range of teaching strategies we are using. If our vision is not in step with current reforms, perhaps the most reasonable staff development plan would be for us to learn more about the reform and to make an explicit decision about whether we want to join in that movement." The other teachers discussed this approach for more than half an hour. Two teachers felt that it would be a waste of time to "study goals again," while one other teacher commented that "the fact that we are disagreeing over whether to study goals might suggest that we don't all agree with each other on what our goals ought to be." Ms. Ward commented that their discussion ought to focus more on some of the other standards and indicators in *Mathematics Programs: A Guide to Evaluation.* "It seems to me that our vision should be aligned with the central part of the vision of mathematics instruction being put forth by the NCTM. We should see if what we want to do is consistent with that vision. I think that Indicators 13.2 and 13.3 would be the most important indicators to focus on as a first step toward understanding our own vision of mathematics instruction. If we don't share that view, then staff development as outlined in Standard 15 might be wasted."

13.2. Teachers create and maintain a classroom atmosphere that supports dialogue and reflection on mathematical understanding.

13.3. Teachers help students learn how to engage in "self-discourse"; that is, ways of interacting with one's own ideas for the purpose of improving those ideas.

Mr. Samuelson said that Ms. Ward's comments were quite helpful. "Staff development has to be about something, so it seems quite useful for staff development to help us improve our vision of mathematics instruction."

After a few more minutes of discussion, the teachers agreed to complete the needs assessment forms for goals and teaching techniques. Mr. James said he would photocopy the forms and put them in teachers' mailboxes. The faculty set a deadline of 1 week to complete the forms and return them to Mrs. Edwards for compiling.

Organizing and Analyzing the Results

Mrs. Edwards agreed to summarize the results. As she reflected on this task, she recognized that it was the discrepancy between perceptions of importance and achievement that would reveal the most important information for planning staff development. She discussed this idea with Mr. James, to see if he could relate how the analysis had been reported at the principals' meeting he attended. He told her that most of the attention at that meeting had been placed on items for which the discrepancy was 2 or more. They agreed to use that technique with the data from teachers at River Bend Elementary.

Because use of a spreadsheet program makes compiling the data a fairly simple task, Mrs. Edwards completed her summary of results in one afternoon during the week after she had received all of the completed forms. She set up the spreadsheet to average the rankings for how important each item was and how much it was currently achieved.

Goals of Instruction

1. Mathematics is presented as a subject to be explored through "what if" situations rather than as a series of facts and algorithms to be memorized.
    importance: 3.7   achievement: 1.7

Teaching Practices

6. Teachers act as facilitators rather than transmitters of knowledge; mathematical ideas are explored with students rather than presented to students.
    importance: 4.5   achievement: 2.4

7. Teachers provide learning tasks that are problematic, that have nonobvious solutions, and that promote "what if" explorations by students and teachers.
    importance: 4.0   achievement: 1.9

Figure 6.2. Items With Greatest Discrepancy

Then she made a summary sheet, which she copied and distributed to the faculty.

At the next faculty meeting, Mrs. Edwards explained that she thought they should focus on the items for which the difference between importance and achievement was 2 or more. There were three such items. One item was in the goals category and two were in the teaching techniques category. (See Figure 6.2.)

Interpretation

Interpreting Results Helps Teachers Grow Professionally

Mr. James asked teachers what they thought the data meant. Ms. Ward commented that "it is important that children be able to use the mathematics that they learn. I hadn't thought much about asking 'what if' questions in elementary school, but I did try out a few with my own students, and, somewhat to my surprise, they could answer the questions and they seemed to enjoy doing so. That probably influenced me most to respond positively to the importance part of those items, even though I am probably not doing a very good job at providing adequate opportunities for students to engage in those types of problems."

Two other teachers commented that, as a result of attending the state mathematics conference last year, they had been trying to explore concepts more with children rather than simply tell children what to learn. They also had been impressed with what the children could accomplish and with the enjoyment that they and their students seemed to get out of these explorations. Those teachers also admitted, however, that they didn't have enough experience with those techniques to feel very successful yet. Ms. Guthrie commented, "These anecdotes seem to reinforce my interpretation of the data that we recognize that there are new ways to teach mathematics, but we are all struggling with how to accomplish those goals. Our staff development plan ought to focus on helping us reach the goals we see as important."

Using the Results

Mr. James then turned the discussion by asking, "What topics should we focus on for a staff development program?" The discussion ranged over several topics: identification of and experience with "what if" situations, problem solving across mathematics content, solving problems in multiple ways, manipulatives as one way to explore mathematics content, facilitating discussion and questioning, and understanding how children learn mathematics so that teachers will better know how to facilitate explorations. Mrs. Edwards commented that one important thread in these ideas was the notion of problem solving. "It seems that we are mainly focusing on how we can become better teachers by using a problem-solving approach. A problem-solving approach can be supported by the use of manipulatives and technology, but that instructional approach would also seem to require a classroom where students feel that it is acceptable to explore ideas, both correct ones and incorrect ones. If we could get some help on learning how to teach using a problem-solving approach, then maybe next year we could return to the problem of evaluating our curriculum using the items in the NCTM book on reviewing school mathematics programs." There was general agreement on this conclusion, so Mr. James raised the question of how many inservice sessions the teachers would be willing to have and how those sessions should be scheduled.

Unusual Suggestions May Be the Most Creative

It became evident early in the discussion that the teachers recognized that staff development on a problem-solving approach to instruction would have to take place over a long period of time. After all, none of the teachers had learned mathematics through problem solving, so they had few models in their memories of teachers that would help them learn this approach. One of the teachers suggested that they should send the children home 1 day a month so that the teachers could have full days of inservice on problem solving. Mr. James said that he didn't think it would be possible to do this in the current year, but he did know of one district in the state that had lengthened each school day by a few minutes so that the children could be dismissed a half day per month. The superintendent and the school board had agreed to this arrangement with the understanding that the time would be used only for teacher inservice. "Maybe we could make a similar proposal to our school board for consideration for next year. But that doesn't solve our immediate problem of trying to decide how much inservice to plan for this year."

The teachers brainstormed ideas, and Mr. James wrote them on the chalkboard: Saturday sessions, monthly or biweekly after-school sessions, and teacher workdays already scheduled. After listening to pros and cons, Mr. Samuelson suggested that they decide on a combination of options. "Probably not everybody is going to be totally happy with the schedule, but we need to have the workshops to improve the instruction to our students." The schedule that they agreed on for the remainder of the school year was three whole-day sessions (one Saturday and two workdays) together with six 2-hour after-school sessions. Mr. James agreed to contact the district's assistant superintendent for instruction to identify a workshop leader and to find the money necessary to pay that person and to buy materials to use in the workshops.

Mr. James understood that the teachers would have to revisit the topic again, after the inservice sessions, to determine how the teachers had changed in their approaches to teaching. Also, he thought that he ought to monitor students' performance on the statewide end-of-year tests to see if the mathematics scores would improve over the next few years. Evaluation is a process that never seems to end!

Summary of Evaluation Principles

There are several important evaluation principles that are illustrated by this vignette.

1. Ideas for evaluation can come from anyone involved in the school, but usually teachers must take charge of focusing the evaluation, because they are most directly involved in instruction. In this case, the idea for conducting a needs assessment came from the principal. Principals are always key players in school buildings; they often set the tone for schools. Principals need to be strong instructional leaders, because they often have a more global view of the instructional strengths and weaknesses of the school as a whole. Whenever evaluation involves instruction, however, teachers need to become heavily involved in planning and carrying out the evaluation. Teachers are the ones with the responsibility for delivering instruction; teachers are the ones that get evaluated first for the quality of instruction in a building. In this vignette, the teacher committee refocused the evaluation as they planned the instrumentation that would be used to gather the data. It was the teachers who recognized that the important first step was to examine the goals and teaching techniques of the faculty.

2. Consider a variety of sources for the evaluation tools. The teachers at River Bend had two main sources of items: the forms distributed by Mr. James and the NCTM book on reviewing programs. On the surface, one might expect the suggestions of a professional organization to be better than the suggestions of a more local project. In this case, however, the items in the NCTM book were viewed as possibly too general and too generic to be of use in this setting. If the evaluation had been aimed at all the schools in a county or in a state, the more general forms might have been better. But the teachers in River Bend wanted information that would be of particular value to them in their particular school.

3. The focus of an evaluation may have to be refined iteratively. Although the initial suggestion of Mr. Samuelson to focus on curriculum seemed like a reasonable one, evaluation of the survey items raised new and more fundamental questions in the minds of the teachers. It is important to keep an open mind about an evaluation as it progresses, because it is always possible that the initial focus of attention is misplaced. Evaluating a mathematics program is analogous to solving a mathematics problem; it is often not clear at the outset what ideas are going to need to be used to complete the evaluation. Evaluators need to be flexible so that, as fundamental underlying concerns become apparent, the evaluation can address those concerns.

4. Keep the target group apprised of the progress of the evaluation and allow them a chance to react to the evaluation strategy. The purpose of the evaluation was to inform the faculty so that decisions could be made about professional development. It was important therefore that the three teachers presented their suggestions about the particular evaluation forms to use, so that the faculty could agree or disagree with those suggestions or could make suggestions for clarifying or redirecting the evaluation. Having the concurrence of the target group prior to conducting the evaluation is critical to the success of the evaluation. Without this concurrence, the faculty could have said that the data were meaningless. Once the faculty agreed with the evaluation strategy, however, there was an investment of the faculty in making significant use of the outcomes of the evaluation.

5. Evaluation is not a simple linear process. There are likely to be many "starts and stops" in an evaluation process, particularly as the focus of the evaluation becomes better clarified and as the evaluation tools are developed. In this vignette, one might assume that the teachers more or less expected that the NCTM book would provide appropriate items to use in the evaluation. After all, such a large professional group has many resources available that would allow them to produce high quality materials. In this case, however, the three teachers decided to take advantage of the evaluation materials that seemed to be better matched to their particular setting.

6. Focus only on a few areas of concern. The faculty could have decided to evaluate all six of the areas outlined in the NCTM book. They realized, however, that some of those areas were more fundamental for an initial evaluation. Other areas could be addressed later.

7. Gather data that will allow decisions to be made. Mr. James's early recognition that the discrepancy between importance and achievement was an important one. It allowed the evaluation to proceed along lines that would generate data that would suggest areas of critical need for professional development. Without gathering both types of data from teachers, the picture might have been distorted, and the faculty might not have been able to reach a clear decision about the substance of an inservice program.

Alternatives to the Strategy Used Here

There are other ways that the data might have been gathered. First, teachers could have been interviewed. This might have made teachers feel like they were "on the spot," and the information they gave might not have been as truthful. Second, teachers could have been asked to list topics that they wanted included in inservice sessions. Such lists are often difficult to summarize, because often the number of topics is quite large, with only a small number of teachers selecting any one of the topics. It is difficult to reach consensus with such data.

Third, Mr. James could have suggested the topics that he felt were important to include in inservice, perhaps based on student performance on the statewide end-of-year tests. Although Mr. James has one view of the state of instruction in River Bend, he is not in the classroom every day working with the children. Consequently, he is not in the best position to know what inservice is needed. Individual teachers, on the other hand, also have biased views. They know their students very well, but they typically know a lot less about the needs of other teachers and of other students. It is important to allow every teacher the chance to have input into the decisions about inservice, but it is important to generate data that will reflect consensus on the needs of all teachers. The evaluation outlined in this vignette meets those criteria.

Cautions Regarding Misinterpretation

It is important the teachers understand that the data do not necessarily suggest that teachers are ready to change in terms of the ways they teach. Rather, the data document only that the teachers seem to recognize a discrepancy between the importance of a problem-solving approach to instruction (e.g., "what if" teaching) and the actual achievement of that style of teaching in the current program. Recognition of a discrepancy is often the first step to change, but teachers are likely to wait until they get more information about problem-solving instruction before they make a deep commitment to particular new ways to teach. That is, the teachers seem ready to consider changing, but the changes themselves will take considerable time to evolve. Both Mr. James and the teachers need to approach the change process with patience but also with a commitment to work on change over a long period of time.

Conclusion

As illustrated in these six vignettes, school personnel can employ relatively simple, straightforward evaluation methods to obtain practical and compelling information to make informed decisions about their school programs. Evaluation results can be used to plan a relevant program, enhance specific program activities, document the impact of these activities, and illustrate the need for and effectiveness of the school mathematics program.

Effective program evaluation is planned and systematic. School personnel in the six vignettes consistently followed a sequence of tasks: focusing the evaluation and identifying the specific evaluation question(s), choosing a method of collecting information that would answer the question(s), planning and carrying out a systematic procedure for collecting information, organizing the information in a summary format, and analyzing and interpreting the data summary to provide answers to the evaluation question(s). Such a step-by-step evaluation plan can help ensure that meaningful results, vital to continued support and improvement of school mathematics programs, are obtained.

Perhaps the most important messages for readers of this guide are the following:

1. School personnel can conduct effective evaluations of their school mathematics programs.
2. By conducting program evaluations, school personnel, including teachers of mathematics, can be convincing advocates for their programs, their students, and themselves.
3. Ongoing evaluations provide vital information to teachers of mathematics and other personnel in their continuous efforts to improve school mathematics programs.

Teachers of mathematics often must take the lead in educating their many and varied audiences of colleagues, administrators, school board members, parents, and others about the significance of their work. We offer this guide to teachers of mathematics and other school personnel as a tool toward empowerment. With the knowledge and skills to conceive, design, and conduct program evaluations, teachers of mathematics and others interested in school mathematics programs can improve their programs, secure additional resources, as well as gain the public support so vital to continued growth.

Resource A:
Standards and Indicators

The first column of the following standards table consists of standards and indicators for effective school mathematics programs. This listing is based on an extensive review of the empirical literature in school mathematics and the NCTM's *Curriculum and Evaluation Standards for School Mathematics* (1989) and the *Professional Standards for Teaching Mathematics* (1991). It is intended to be a guide for evaluating school mathematics programs.

Because it would be expensive and time consuming to evaluate every indicator of a standard at the same time, it is suggested that evaluations be narrowed to one or two indicators. First, locate the heading ("Content Standards," "Teaching Standards," or "Assessment Standards") that best describes the general area of interest for an upcoming evaluation. Next, select a standard within an area. For example, within the content area, one might select "mathematics as problem solving" or "mathematics as communication."

Once the standard for evaluation has been selected, choose the indicators that seem most appropriate and feasible for your specific evaluation question. For example, assume that you are interested in the standard "Mathematics as Problem Solving." Is your interest in assessing whether students have opportunities to develop and carry out plans to solve a wide variety of routine and nonroutine problems (Indicator 1.3) or in determining whether students have opportunities to define problems in both everyday life and mathematical situations (Indicator 1.2)?

The second column of the standards table lists possible evaluation methods that are appropriate to each indicator listed. If you choose Indicator 1.3 for evaluation, then you would find analysis of teacher lesson plans and student work in the adjacent column. Several of the evaluation methods listed in the second column are illustrated in the vignettes that constitute the core of this guide. A key to these six vignettes and to the methods of evaluation is located in the third column of the

108

standards table. For example, the evaluation methods appropriate to Indicator 1.3 are illustrated in Vignette 1.

Standards and Indicators	Evaluation Methods	Key to Vignettes
CONTENT STANDARDS		
Standard 1. Mathematics as Problem Solving		
1.1. Students have opportunities to solve problems on a regular basis.	Inspection of lesson plans (checklist) Interviews of students	1
1.2. Students have opportunities to define problems in both everyday life and mathematical situations.	Inspection of student work (checklist)	1, 5
1.3. Students have opportunities to develop and carry out plans to solve a wide variety of routine and nonroutine problems, to look back at the original problems to verify and interpret their results, and to generalize solutions and strategies to other situations.	Inspection of lesson plans (checklist) Inspection of student work (checklist) Interviews of students Student questionnaire	1 1, 5
1.4. Students have opportunities to acquire confidence in their ability to use mathematics to solve problems.	Student questionnaire Interviews of students	
Standard 2. Mathematics as Communication		
2.1. Students have opportunities to relate physical materials, pictures, and diagrams to mathematical ideas, with increasing emphasis on graphing and algebraic methods as the students mature.	Inspection of student work (checklist) Observation during instruction	1, 5
2.2. Students have opportunities to develop common understandings of mathematical ideas, with increasing emphasis on definitions, conjectures, arguments, and generalizations as the students mature.	Interviews of students Inspection of student work (checklist) Observation during instruction	1, 5
2.3. Students have opportunities to ask clarifying questions related to mathematics situations they have read or heard about.	Observation during instruction	
Standard 3. Mathematics as Reasoning		
3.1. Students have opportunities to use models, known facts, properties, and relationships to explain their thinking.	Interviews of students Inspection of student work (checklist) Observation during instruction Experiment	1,5 5
3.2. Students have opportunities to justify their answers and solution processes.	Inspection of student work (checklist) Observation during instruction	1, 5

Standards and Indicators	Evaluation Methods	Key to Vignettes
3.3. Students have opportunities to draw logical conclusions about mathematics and to recognize and apply deductive and inductive reasoning.	Inspection of student work (checklist) Observation during instruction	1, 5
3.4. Students have opportunities to make and evaluate mathematical conjectures and arguments.	Inspection of student work (checklist) Observation during instruction	1, 5
3.5. Students have opportunities to formulate counterexamples.	Inspection of student work (checklist) Observation during instruction Interviews of students	1, 5
3.6. Students have opportunities to develop an appreciation of the pervasive use and power of reasoning as a part of mathematics.	Inspection of student work (checklist) Observation during instruction	1, 5
Standard 4. Mathematical Connections		
4.1. Students have opportunities to link conceptual and procedural knowledge within mathematics.	Inspection of student work (checklist) Observation during instruction Interviews of students	1, 5
4.2. Students have opportunities to relate various representations of concepts or procedures to one another.	Inspection of student work (checklist) Observation during instruction Experiment	1, 5 5
4.3. Students have opportunities to recognize and value relationships among different topics in mathematics.	Inspection of student work (checklist) Observation during instruction	1, 5
4.4. Students have opportunities to explore and describe results using graphic, numerical, physical, algebraic, and verbal models or representations.	Inspection of student work (checklist) Observation during instruction Experiment	1, 5 5
4.5. Students have opportunities to apply and value mathematical thinking and modeling to solve problems that arise in other disciplines, such as art, music, psychology, science, and business.	Inspection of student work (checklist) Observation during instruction Experiment	1, 5 5
Standard 5. Number, Numeration, and Computation		
5.1. Students have opportunities to develop increasingly sophisticated concepts about numbers (i.e., whole numbers, integers, common and decimal fractions, irrational and complex numbers) and to understand and appreciate the need for numbers beyond the whole numbers.	Inspection of student work (checklist) Observation during instruction Content analysis of instructional materials	1, 5 3, 4

Standards and Indicators	Evaluation Methods	Key to Vignettes
5.2. Students have opportunities to construct number meanings through real-world experience and the use of physical materials, to understand counting, grouping, and place-value concepts, to develop and use order relations for numbers, and to interpret the multiple uses of numbers in the real world.	Inspection of student work (checklist) Observation during instruction Interviews of students Inspection of lesson plans (checklist) Experiment	1, 5 1 5
5.3. Students have opportunities to explore estimation strategies, including recognizing when estimation is appropriate or inappropriate, determining reasonableness of results, and applying estimation in working with quantities, measurement, computation, and problem solving.	Inspection of student work (checklist) Observation during instruction Inspection of lesson plans (checklist) Content analysis of instructional materials	1, 5 1 3, 4
5.4. Students have opportunities to understand how the basic arithmetic operations are related to one another.	Inspection of student work (checklist) Observation during instruction Interviews of students Content analysis of instructional materials	1, 5 3, 4
5.5. Students have opportunities to acquire reasonable proficiency with basic facts and algorithms, including those for whole numbers, fractions, decimals, integers, and rational numbers and to use a variety of mental computation and estimation techniques.	Inspection of student work (checklist) Observation during instruction Interviews of students Achievement test scores	 1, 5 2
5.6. Students have opportunities to learn how to select and use computational techniques appropriate to specific problems, including the use of calculators of various types.	Inspection of student work (checklist) Observation during instruction Interviews of students Inspection of lesson plans (checklist) Content analysis of instructional materials	1,5 1 3, 4
Standard 6. Patterns and Functions		
6.1. Students have opportunities to recognize, describe, extend, and create a wide variety of patterns and to use patterns to analyze mathematical situations.	Inspection of student work (checklist) Observation during instruction Interviews of students	1, 5
6.2. Students have opportunities to explore the use of variables, open sentences, tables, graphs, verbal rules, and equations to describe and express relationships.	Inspection of student work (checklist) Observation during instruction Interviews of students Inspection of lesson plans (checklist)	1, 5 1

Standards and Indicators	Evaluation Methods	Key to Vignettes
	Content analysis of instructional materials	3, 4
6.3. Students have opportunities to analyze functional relationships to explain how a change in one quantity results in a change in another.	Inspection of student work (checklist) Observation during instruction Interviews of students Content analysis of instructional materials	1, 5 3, 4
6.4. Students have opportunities to model real-world phenomena with a variety of functions.	Inspection of student work (checklist) Interviews of students Observation during instruction Inspection of lesson plans (checklist)	1, 5 1
6.5. Students have opportunities to recognize that a variety of problem situations can be modeled by the same type of function.	Inspection of student work (checklist) Interviews of students Observation during instruction	1, 5
Standard 7. Measurement		
7.1. Students have opportunities to develop the process of measuring and developing concepts related to units of measurement as well as the process of measurement.	Inspection of student work (checklist) Observation during instruction Interviews of students	1, 5
7.2. Students have opportunities to select units and tools of measure appropriate for the degree of accuracy required in a particular situation.	Inspection of student work (checklist) Observation during instruction Interviews of students Inspection of lesson plans (checklist)	1, 5 1
7.3. Students have opportunities to acquire concepts of length, capacity, weight, mass, area, volume, perimeter, time, temperature, and angle.	Inspection of student work (checklist) Observation during instruction Interviews of students Achievement test scores Content analysis of instructional materials Inspection of lesson plans (checklist)	1, 5 2 3, 4 1
7.4. Students have opportunities to understand the structure and use of systems of measurement.	Inspection of student work (checklist) Observation during instruction Interviews of students	1, 5

Standards and Indicators	Evaluation Methods	Key to Vignettes
7.5. Students have opportunities to develop formulas and procedures for determining measures to solve problems.	Inspection of student work (checklist) Observation during instruction Interviews of students Content analysis of instructional materials Achievement test scores	1, 5 3, 4 2
Standard 8. Statistics and Data Analysis		
8.1. Students have opportunities to systematically collect, organize, and describe data.	Inspection of student work (checklist) Interviews of students Observation during instruction Content analysis of instructional materials Inspection of lesson plans (checklist)	1, 5 3, 4 1
8.2. Students have opportunities to construct, read, and interpret tables, charts, graphs.	Inspection of student work (checklist) Interviews of students Observation during instruction Content analysis of instructional materials Inspection of lesson plans (checklist)	1, 5 3, 4 1
8.3. Students have opportunities to formulate and solve problems that involve collecting and analyzing data.	Inspection of student work (checklist) Interviews of students Observation during instruction Inspection of lesson plans (checklist)	1, 5 1
8.4. Students have opportunities to make inferences and convincing arguments that are based on data analysis and to develop an appreciation for statistical methods as powerful means for decision making	Inspection of student work (checklist) Interviews of students Observation during instruction	1, 5
8.5. Students have opportunities to understand and apply measures of central tendency, variability, and correlation.	Inspection of student work (checklist) Interviews of students Observation during instruction Achievement test scores Inspection of lesson plans (checklist)	1, 5 2 1

Standards and Indicators	*Evaluation Methods*	*Key to Vignettes*
Standard 9. Geometry and Spatial Reasoning		
9.1. Students have opportunities to identify, describe, model, draw, and classify two-dimensional and three-dimensional shapes and geometric figures.	Inspection of student work (checklist)	1, 5
	Interviews of students	
	Observation during instruction	
	Inspection of lesson plans (checklist)	1
	Achievement test scores	2
	Content analysis of instructional materials	3, 4
	Experiment	5
9.2. Students have opportunities to visualize and represent geometric figures and to develop spatial sense.	Inspection of student work (checklist)	1, 5
	Interviews of students	
	Observation during instruction	
9.3. Students have opportunities to classify figures in terms of congruence and similarity and apply these relationships.	Inspection of student work (checklist)	1, 5
	Interviews of students	
	Observation during instruction	
	Inspection of lesson plans (checklist)	1
9.4. Students have opportunities to explore transformations of geometric figures and to deduce properties of figures using transformations and coordinates.	Inspection of student work (checklist)	1, 5
	Interviews of students	
	Observation during instruction	
9.5. Students have opportunities to analyze properties of Euclidean transformations and relate translations to vectors.	Inspection of student work (checklist)	1, 5
	Interviews of students	
	Observation during instruction	
	Inspection of lesson plans (checklist)	1
9.6. Students have opportunities to relate geometric ideas to number and measurement ideas and to recognize and appreciate geometry in their world.	Inspection of student work (checklist)	1, 5
	Interviews of students	
	Observation during instruction	
Standard 10. Algebra		
10.1. Students have opportunities to understand the concepts of variable, expression, and equation.	Inspection of student work (checklist)	1, 5
	Interviews of students	
	Observation during instruction	
	Inspection of lesson plans (checklist)	1
	Achievement test scores	2
	Content analysis of instructional materials	3, 4

Standards and Indicators	Evaluation Methods	Key to Vignettes
10.2. Students have opportunities to represent situations and number patterns with tables, graphs, verbal rules, expressions, equations, and inequalities and explore the interrelationships of these representations.	Inspection of student work (checklist) Interviews of students Observation during instruction Inspection of lesson plans (checklist)	1, 5 1
10.3. Students have opportunities to develop confidence in solving linear equations using concrete, informal, and formal methods.	Inspection of student work (checklist) Interviews of students Observation during instruction	1, 5
10.4. Students have opportunities to apply algebraic methods to solve a variety of real-world and mathematical problems.	Inspection of student work (checklist) Interviews of students Observation during instruction Inspection of lesson plans (checklist)	1, 5 1
10.5. Students have opportunities to study mathematical structures.	Inspection of student work (checklist) Interviews of students Observation during instruction	1, 5
10.6. Students have opportunities to study trigonometry and the conceptual underpinnings of calculus.	Inspection of lesson plans (checklist) Inspection of student work (checklist) Interviews of students Observation during instruction	1 1, 5
Standard 11. Probability and Discrete Mathematics		
11.1. Students have opportunities to understand the concepts of probability, sample space, event, outcome, and so on through experience with probability experiments (e.g., rolling dice, spinning spinners) and with computer simulations of experiments.	Inspection of student work (checklist) Interviews of students Observation during instruction Achievement test scores Experiment	1, 5 2 5
11.2. Students have opportunities to develop confidence in analyzing probabilistic situations using both formal and informal methods.	Inspection of student work (checklist) Interviews of students Observation during instruction	1, 5
11.3. Students have opportunities to develop an appreciation for the power of using probability models by comparing experimental results with mathematical expectations and for the pervasive use of probability in the real world.	Inspection of student work (checklist) Interviews of students Observation during instruction	1, 5

Standards and Indicators	Evaluation Methods	Key to Vignettes
11.4. Students have opportunities to study discrete mathematics.	Inspection of lesson plans (checklist)	1
TEACHING STANDARDS		
Standard 12. Worthwhile Mathematical Tasks		
12.1. Teachers provide a wide range of mathematical tasks that are appropriate for the age and developmental level of students and that engage students' interests.	Inspection of lesson plans (checklist)	1
	Content analysis of instructional materials	3, 4
	Teacher questionnaire (survey)	3, 4, 6
	Focus group	3
	Experiment	5
12.2. Teachers select mathematical tasks that reflect the full range of mathematics content and that support connections between mathematics and other disciplines.	Inspection of lesson plans (checklist)	1
	Content analysis of instructional materials	3, 4
	Teacher questionnaire (survey)	3, 4, 6
	Focus group	3
12.3. Teachers are familiar with sources of appropriate mathematical tasks.	Teacher questionnaire (survey)	3, 4, 6
	Focus group	3
12.4. Teachers allow students sufficient time to be engaged with tasks so that understanding of the relevant mathematics can be acquired.	Observation during instruction	1
	Inspection of lesson plans (checklist)	
	Interviews of students	
Standard 13. Mathematical Discourse		
13.1. Teachers and students engage in significant mathematical discourse, both orally and in writing.	Observation during instruction	
	Interviews of students	
13.2. Teachers create and maintain a classroom atmosphere that supports dialogue and reflection on mathematical understanding.	Observation during instruction	
	Inventory of school facilities	3
13.3. Teachers help students learn how to engage in "self-discourse"; that is, ways of interacting with one's own ideas for the purpose of improving those ideas.	Interviews of students	
Standard 14. Learning Environment		
14.1. Teachers create a positive learning environment.	Observation during instruction	
	Interviews of students	
14.2. Instructional activities are based on students' previous mathematical experiences, are planned to lead students	Observation during instruction	
	Interviews of students	
	Inspection of lesson plans	1

Standards and Indicators	Evaluation Methods	Key to Vignettes
from the concrete to the abstract, and regularly include problem solving.	(checklist) Teacher interview	
14.3. Remedial instruction is provided when needed.	Teacher interview Inspection of lesson plans (checklist) Inspection of student work (checklist)	1 1, 5
14.4. The needs of exceptional students are addressed in terms of accessible instructional space, supportive equipment, and appropriate instruction.	Observation during instruction Teacher questionnaire (survey)	3, 4, 6
14.5. Teachers of mathematics meet current requirements for certification.	Teacher questionnaire (survey) Analysis of district records	3, 4, 6 2
14.6. Instructional areas have visual, climatic, and acoustic qualities that contribute to learning.	Observation during instruction Teacher questionnaire (survey)	3, 4, 6
14.7. Teachers are given an inventory of available manipulatives (e.g., geoboards) and supplementary instructional materials (e.g., videotapes); materials in adequate variety and sufficient quantity are easily accessible; materials are matched with the instructional program; and materials are used by students in learning.	Teacher interview Teacher questionnaire (survey) Focus group Inventory of school facilities	3, 4, 6 3 3
14.8. Equipment (e.g., calculators, computers, overhead projectors, and so on) to support the mathematics program is readily available and securely stored.	Teacher interview Focus group Inventory of school facilities	3 3
Standard 15. Teacher Enhancement		
15.1. Teachers of mathematics participate in ongoing mathematics inservice programs, college-level programs, institutes, and conferences.	Teacher questionnaire (survey) Analysis of district records	3, 4, 6 2
15.2. Provisions are made for teachers to meet with each other to share concerns, confer about individual students, and plan mathematics and interdisciplinary programs.	Focus group Teacher questionnaire (survey) Teacher interview	3 3, 4, 6
15.3. Publications and materials from professional mathematics organizations are available in the school, and a mathematics resource area is available to teachers.	Teacher questionnaire (survey) Inventory of school facilities	3, 4, 6 3
15.4. The principal provides instructional leadership and support for the mathematics program.	Teacher interview Teacher questionnaire (survey)	3, 4, 6

Standards and Indicators	*Evaluation Methods*	*Key to Vignettes*
15.5. Mathematics teachers have input into the planning of new or renovated facilities.	Teacher questionnaire (survey) Teacher interview Focus group	3, 4, 6 3
15.6. Teachers have input into selection of textbooks, supplemental materials for the classroom, and materials collections in libraries or media centers.	Teacher questionnaire (survey) Teacher interview Focus group	3, 4, 6 3

ASSESSMENT STANDARDS

Standard 16.   Mathematical Power

16.1. Students know and can use mathematics concepts, procedures, and problem-solving strategies appropriate to a given situation.	Achievement test scores Observation during instruction Interviews of students Inspection of student work (checklist)	2 1, 5
16.2. Students have opportunities to develop an appreciation for the use of mathematics in a variety of real-world settings.	Observation during instruction Interviews of students Inspection of student work (checklist)	 1, 5

Standard 17.   Mathematical Disposition

17.1. Student assessments measure confidence in, and perseverance for, using mathematics to solve problems, to communicate ideas, and to reason.	Teacher interview Focus group Teacher questionnaire (survey) Content analysis of assessment instruments	 3 3, 4, 6
17.2. Student assessments measure flexibility, interest, curiosity, and inventiveness in exploring mathematical ideas and trying alternative methods in solving problems.	Teacher interview Focus group Teacher questionnaire (survey) Content analysis of assessment instruments	 3 3, 4, 6
17.3. Student assessments measure inclination to monitor and reflect on their own thinking and performance.	Teacher interview Focus group Teacher questionnaire (survey) Content analysis of assessment instruments	 3 3, 4, 6
17.4. Student assessments measure valuing of the application of mathematics to situations arising in other disciplines and everyday experiences.	Teacher interview Focus group Teacher questionnaire (survey) Content analysis of assessment instruments	 3 3, 4, 6

Standards and Indicators	Evaluation Methods	Key to Vignettes
17.5. Student assessments measure appreciation of the role of mathematics in our culture and its value as a tool and as a language.	Teacher interview Focus group Teacher questionnaire (survey) Content analysis of assessment instruments	 3 3, 4, 6
17.6. Counselors and mathematics teachers maintain effective communication for advising students about program decisions and for planning of instructional schedules.	Teacher questionnaire (survey) Focus group Teacher interview Analysis of district records	3, 4, 6 3 2
Standard 18. Alignment		
18.1. Lesson plans and actual class instruction are based on accepted learning objectives, and students are aware of the objectives of each lesson.	Inspection of lesson plans (checklist) Observation during instruction Interviews of students Student questionnaire	1
18.2. Student assessments are aligned with the goals, objectives, and mathematical content of the curriculum and with instructional approaches (e.g., use of calculators, computers, and manipulatives) used by teachers.	Content analysis of assessment instruments	
18.3. Teaching practices include use of different grouping strategies (i.e., large group, small group, individual) and appropriate manipulatives and technologies.	Inspection of lesson plans (checklist) Observation during instruction Experiment	1 5
18.4. Instruction is adapted in terms of pacing and learning styles to match the students and the content.	Observation during instruction Experiment	5
18.5. Procedures are established to evaluate the appropriateness and effectiveness of the mathematics program, with results of the evaluation used to make necessary modifications.	Teacher interview Focus group	 3
18.6. Teachers, staff, members of the community, school system consultants, and outside consultants are periodically involved in developing and evaluating the mathematics program.	Teacher questionnaire (survey) Teacher interview Staff interviews Analysis of district's long-term goals	3, 4, 6
Standard 19. Multiple Sources of Information		
19.1. Assessment methods that demand different kinds of mathematical thinking are used.	Teacher interview Teacher questionnaire (survey) Focus group	 3, 4, 6 3

Standards and Indicators	Evaluation Methods	Key to Vignettes
	Content analysis of assessment instruments	
19.2. Assessment tools that present the same mathematical concept or procedure in different contexts, formats, and problem situations are used.	Teacher interview Teacher questionnaire (survey) Focus group Content analysis of assessment instruments	3, 4, 6 3
Standard 20. Appropriate Assessment Methods and Uses		
20.1. Different assessment procedures are used to measure understanding of concepts, procedures, and problem solving.	Content analysis of assessment instruments Focus group Teacher interview	3
20.2. Appropriate diagnostic measures and tools are available to assess student needs and are used for prescribing appropriate instructional activities for individual students.	Content analysis of assessment instruments Focus group Teacher interview	3
20.3. Teachers use acceptable methods for recording students' progress.	Teacher questionnaire (survey) Focus group Teacher interview	3, 4, 6 3
20.4. Teachers provide consistent evaluation and interpretation of student progress.	Experiment Parent questionnaires (survey) Teacher questionnaire (survey) Focus group Teacher interview	5 3, 4, 6 3
20.5. Communication of student progress to students and parents is effective.	Teacher questionnaire (survey) Focus group Teacher interview	3, 4, 6 3

Resource B:
Bibliography of Selected
References

Resource B consists of a list of references that have been selected to provide the reader with additional examples and explanations of concerns critical to the evaluation of mathematics programs. The articles, chapters, and books have been organized around four categories: general, assessment/evaluation, curriculum, and teaching. We hope that these references will be helpful as evaluation questions are discussed, posed, and tested.

Entries in the "general" and "assessment/evaluation" categories outline overarching concerns that teachers should be aware of in interpreting any type of mathematics program. What do we know in general about the effectiveness of mathematics instruction over the past 50 years? Why does an understanding of learning theory help frame appropriate questions for evaluation? What mathematics is needed for people in the twenty-first century?

Entries in the "curriculum" category shed light on the nature of the mathematics curriculum. What is appropriate content for algebra or for geometry? What is the vision of mathematics curriculum for kindergarten through Grade 12? What do we know about how students learn problem-solving skills?

Entries in the "teaching" category deal with strategies for engaging students in the learning of mathematics. How do teachers support discourse in a classroom? What is the student's role in a classroom where discourse is valued? How can manipulatives or technology be used to teach mathematics content? What are effective ways to teach problem solving?

General

Glennon, V. J., & Callahan, L. C. (1986). *A guide to current research: Elementary school mathematics*. Washington, DC: Association for Supervision and Curriculum Development.

Kearns, D. T., & Doyle, D. P. (1986). *Winning the brain race*. San Francisco: Institute for Contemporary Studies.

Larkin, J. H. (1989). Eight reasons for explicit theories in mathematics education. In S. Wagner & C. Kieran (Eds.), *Research issues in the learning and teaching of algebra* (pp. 275-277). Hillsdale, NJ: Lawrence Erlbaum.

National Council of Supervisors of Mathematics. (1988). *Essential mathematics for the 21st century*. Reston, VA: Author.

Pollack, H. O. (1983). *Educating Americans for the 21st century: A plan of action for improving mathematics, science and technology education for all American elementary and secondary students so that their achievement is the best in the world by 1995*. Washington, DC: National Science Board Commission on Precollege Education in Mathematics, Science, and Technology.

Research Advisory Committee of the National Council of Teachers of Mathematics. (1989). *Setting a research agenda*. Hillsdale, NJ: Lawrence Erlbaum.

Steen, L. (1989). *Everybody counts: A report to the nation on the future of mathematics education*. Washington, DC: National Academy Press.

Assessment/Evaluation

Blume, G. W., & Nicely, R. F., Jr. (1991). *A guide for reviewing school mathematics programs*. Reston, VA: National Council of Teachers of Mathematics.

Campione, J. C., Brown, A. L., & Connell, M. L. (1988). Metacognition: On the importance of understanding what you are doing. In R. I. Charles & E. A. Silver (Eds.), *The teaching and assessing of mathematical problem solving* (pp. 93-114). Hillsdale, NJ: Lawrence Erlbaum.

Chaiklin, S. (1989). Cognitive studies of algebra problem solving and learning. In S. Wagner & C. Kieran (Eds.), *Research issues in the learning and teaching of algebra* (pp. 93-114). Hillsdale, NJ: Lawrence Erlbaum.

Charles, R., Lester, F., & O'Daffer, P. (1987). *How to evaluate progress in problem solving*. Reston, VA: National Council of Teachers of Mathematics.

Davis, R. B. (1989). Three ways of improving cognitive studies in algebra. In S. Wagner & C. Kieran (Eds.), *Research issues in the learning and teaching of algebra* (pp. 115-119). Hillsdale, NJ: Lawrence Erlbaum.

Dossey, J. A., Mullis, I. V. S, Lindquist, M. M., & Chambers, D. L. (1988). *The mathematics report card: Are we measuring up?* Princeton, NJ: Educational Testing Service.

Fennema, E. (1981). The sex factor. In E. Fennema (Ed.), *Mathematics education research: Implications for the '80s* (pp. 92-104). Alexandria, VA: Association for Supervision and Curriculum Development.

Fraser, B. J., Malone, J. S., & Neale, J. M. (1989). Assessing and improving the psychosocial environment of mathematics classrooms. *Journal for Research in Mathematics Education, 20,* 191-201.

Lester, F. K., Jr. (1988). Reflections about mathematical problem-solving research. In R. I. Charles & E. A. Silver (Eds.), *The teaching and assessing of mathematical problem solving* (pp. 115-124). Hillsdale, NJ: Lawrence Erlbaum.

Marshall, S. P. (1988). Assessing problem solving: A short-term remedy and a long-term solution. In R. I. Charles & E. A. Silver (Eds.), *The teaching and assessing of mathematical problem solving* (pp. 159-177). Hillsdale, NJ: Lawrence Erlbaum.

Mauer, S. B. (1987). New knowledge about errors and new views about learners: What they mean to educators and more educators would like to know. In A. H. Schoenfeld (Ed.), *Cognitive science and mathematics education* (pp. 165-188). Hillsdale, NJ: Lawrence Erlbaum.

National Council of Teachers of Mathematics. (1987). *How to evaluate your mathematics program.* Reston, VA: Author.

Research Advisory Committee of the National Council of Teachers of Mathematics. (1984). A plan for assessing the impact of the NCTM's agenda for action. *Journal for Research in Mathematics Education, 15,* 3-14.

Schoenfeld, A. H. (1988). Problem solving in context(s). In R. I. Charles & E. A. Silver (Eds.), *The teaching and assessing of mathematical problem solving* (pp. 82-92). Hillsdale, NJ: Lawrence Erlbaum.

Silver, E. A. (1988). Teaching and assessing mathematical problem solving: Toward a research agenda. In R. I. Charles & E. A. Silver (Eds.), *The teaching and assessing of mathematical problem solving* (pp. 273-282). Hillsdale, NJ: Lawrence Erlbaum.

Silver, E. A., & Kilpatrick, J. (1988). Testing mathematical problem solving. In R. I. Charles & E. A. Silver (Eds.), *The teaching and assessing of mathematical problem solving* (pp. 178-186). Hillsdale, NJ: Lawrence Erlbaum.

Stigler, J. W., & Perry, M. (1988). Cross-cultural studies of mathematics teaching and learning: Recent findings and new directions. In D. A. Grouws, T. J. Cooney, & D. Jones (Eds.), *Effective mathematics teaching* (pp. 194-223). Hillsdale, NJ: Lawrence Erlbaum.

Sueltz, B. A. (1961). The role of evaluation in the classroom. In *Evaluation in mathematics: Twenty-sixth yearbook* (pp. 7-21). Washington, DC: National Council of Teachers of Mathematics.

Thompson, P. W. (1989). Artificial intelligence, advanced technology, and learning and teaching algebra. In S. Wagner & C. Kieran (Eds.), *Research issues in the learning and teaching of algebra* (pp. 135-161). Hillsdale, NJ: Lawrence Erlbaum.

Thorpe, J. (1989). Algebra: What should we teach and how should we teach it? In S. Wagner & C. Kieran (Eds.), *Research issues in the learning and teaching of algebra* (pp. 11-24). Hillsdale, NJ: Lawrence Erlbaum.

Curriculum

Baroody, A. J. (1987). *Children's mathematical thinking.* New York: Teachers College Press.

Blume, G. W., & Schoen, H. L. (1988). Mathematical problem-solving performance of eighth-grade programmers and nonprogrammers. *Journal for Research in Mathematics Education, 19,* 142-156.

Booth, L. R. (1989). A question of structure. In S. Wagner & C. Kieran (Eds.), *Research issues in the learning and teaching of algebra* (pp. 57-59). Hillsdale, NJ: Lawrence Erlbaum.

Bransford, J., Hasselbring, T., Barron, B., Kulewicz, S., Littlefield, J., & Goin, L. (1988). Uses of macro-contexts to facilitate mathematical thinking. In R. I. Charles & E. A. Silver (Eds.), *The teaching and assessing of mathematical problem solving* (pp. 125-147). Hillsdale, NJ: Lawrence Erlbaum.

Burton, L. (1984). Mathematical thinking: The struggle for meaning. *Journal for Research in Mathematics Education, 15,* 35-49.

Carpenter, T. P., Moser, J. M., & Romberg, T. A. (Eds.). (1982). *Addition and subtraction: A cognitive perspective.* Hillsdale, NJ: Lawrence Erlbaum.

Carraher, T. N., Carraher, D. W., & Schliemann, A. D. (1987). Written and oral mathematics. *Journal for Research in Mathematics Education, 18,* 83-97.

Case, R. (1989). Summary comments: Developing a research agenda for mathematics in the middle grades. In J. Hiebert & M. Behr (Eds.), *Number concepts and operations in the middle grades* (pp. 265-270). Hillsdale, NJ: Lawrence Erlbaum.

Chaiklin, S. (1989). Cognitive studies of algebra problem solving and learning. In S. Wagner & C. Kieran (Eds.), *Research issues in the learning and teaching of algebra* (pp. 93-114). Hillsdale, NJ: Lawrence Erlbaum.

Conference Board of the Mathematical Sciences. (1984). *New goals for mathematical sciences education.* Washington, DC: Author.

Crosswhite, F. J. (1987). Cognitive science and mathematics education: A mathematics educator's perspective. In A. H. Schoenfeld (Ed.), *Cognitive science and mathematics education* (pp. 265-278). Hillsdale. NJ: Lawrence Erlbaum.

Davis, R. B. (1989). Research studies in how humans think about algebra. In S. Wagner & C. Kieran (Eds.), *Research issues in the learning and teaching of algebra* (pp. 266-274). Hillsdale, NJ: Lawrence Erlbaum.

Dessart, D. J. (1981). Curriculum. In E. Fennema (Ed.), *Mathematics education research: Implications for the '80s* (pp. 1-21). Alexandria, VA: Association for Supervision and Curriculum Development.

DeVault, M. (1981). Computers. In E. Fennema (Ed.), *Mathematics education research: Implications for the '80s* (pp. 131-148). Alexandria, VA: Association for Supervision and Curriculum Development.

Fey, J. T. (1989). School algebra for the year 2000. In S. Wagner & C. Kieran (Eds.), *Research issues in the learning and teaching of algebra* (pp. 199-213). Hillsdale, NJ: Lawrence Erlbaum.

Fuson, K. (1989). Summary comments: Meaning in middle grade number concepts. In J. Hiebert & M. Behr (Eds.), *Number concepts and operations in the middle grades* (pp. 260-264). Hillsdale, NJ: Lawrence Erlbaum.

Ginsberg, H. P. (Ed.). (1983). *The development of mathematical thinking.* New York: Academic Press.

Greeno, J. G. (1978). A study of problem solving. In R. Glaser (Ed.), *Advances in instructional psychology* (Vol. 1, pp. 13-75). Hillsdale, NJ: Lawrence Erlbaum.

Greeno, J. G. (1988). For the study of mathematics epistemology. In R. I. Charles & E. A. Silver (Eds.), *The teaching and assessing of mathematical problem solving* (pp. 23-31). Hillsdale, NJ: Lawrence Erlbaum.

Hart, K. (1989). Ratio and proportion. In J. Hiebert & M. Behr (Eds.), *Number concepts and operations in the middle grades* (pp. 198-219). Hillsdale, NJ: Lawrence Erlbaum.

Hiebert, J. (Ed.). (1986). *Conceptual and procedural knowledge: The case of mathematics.* Hillsdale, NJ: Lawrence Erlbaum.

Kieran, C. (1989). The early learning of algebra: A structural perspective. In S. Wagner & C. Kieran (Eds.), *Research issues in the learning and teaching of algebra* (pp. 33-56). Hillsdale, NJ: Lawrence Erlbaum.

Kieren, T. E. (1989). Personal knowledge of rational numbers: Its intuitive and formal development. In J. Hiebert & M. Behr (Eds.), *Number concepts and operations in the middle grades* (pp. 162-181). Hillsdale, NJ: Lawrence Erlbaum.

Kilpatrick, J. (1987). Problem formulating: Where do good problems come from? In A. H. Schoenfeld (Ed.), *Cognitive science and mathematics education* (pp. 123-148). Hillsdale, NJ: Lawrence Erlbaum.

Lesh, R., Post, T., & Behr, M. (1989). Proportional reasoning. In J. Hiebert & M. Behr (Eds.), *Number concepts and operations in the middle grades* (pp. 93-118). Hillsdale, NJ: Lawrence Erlbaum.

Lester, F. K., Jr., & Garofalo, J. (Eds.). (1982). *Mathematical problem solving: Issues in research.* Philadelphia: Franklin Institute Press.

Lewis, M. W. (1989). The research agenda in algebra: A cognitive science perspective. In S. Wagner & C. Kieran (Eds.), *Research issues in the learning and teaching of algebra* (pp. 247-256). Hillsdale, NJ: Lawrence Erlbaum.

McLeod, D. B. (1988). Affective issues in mathematical problem solving: Some theoretical considerations. *Journal for Research in Mathematics Education, 19,* 134-141.

Moyer, J. C., Moyer, B., Sowder, L., & Threadgill-Sowder, J. (1984). Story problem formats: Verbal versus telegraphic. *Journal for Research in Mathematics Education, 15,* 64-68.

National Council of Teachers of Mathematics. (1989). *Curriculum and evaluation standards for school mathematics.* Reston, VA: Author.

Nesher, P. (1989). Multiplicative school word problems: Theoretical approaches and empirical findings. In J. Hiebert & M. Behr (Eds.), *Number concepts and operations in the middle grades* (pp. 19-40). Hillsdale, NJ: Lawrence Erlbaum.

Ohlsson, S. (1989). Mathematical meaning and applicational meaning in the semantics of fractions and related concepts. In J. Hiebert & M. Behr (Eds.), *Number concepts and operations in the middle grades* (pp. 53-92). Hillsdale, NJ: Lawrence Erlbaum.

Owen, E., & Sweller, J. (1989). Should problem solving be used as a learning device in mathematics? *Journal for Research in Mathematics Education, 20,* 322-327.

Pea, R. D. (1987). Cognitive technologies for mathematics education. In A. H. Schoenfeld (Ed.), *Cognitive science and mathematics education* (pp. 89-122). Hillsdale, NJ: Lawrence Erlbaum.

Pollack, H. O. (1987). Cognitive science and mathematics education: A mathematician's perspective. In A. H. Schoenfeld (Ed.), *Cognitive science and mathematics education* (pp. 253-264). Hillsdale, NJ: Lawrence Erlbaum.

Porter, A., Floden, R., Freeman, I. D., Schmidt, W., & Schwille, J. (1988). Content determinants in elementary school mathematics. In D. A. Grouws, T. J. Cooney, & D. Jones (Eds.), *Effective mathematics teaching* (pp. 96-113). Hillsdale, NJ: Lawrence Erlbaum.

Rachlin, S. L. (1989). The research agenda in algebra: A curriculum perspective. In S. Wagner & C. Kieran (Eds.), *Research issues in the learning and teaching of algebra* (pp. 257-265). Hillsdale, NJ: Lawrence Erlbaum.

Research Advisory Committee of the National Council of Teachers of Mathematics. (1986). NCTM curriculum and evaluation standards for school mathematics: Responses from the research community. *Journal for Research in Mathematics Education, 19,* 338-344.

Resnick, L. B. (1988). Treating mathematics as an ill-structured discipline. In R. I. Charles & E. A. Silver (Eds.), *The teaching and assessing of mathematical problem solving* (pp. 32-60). Hillsdale, NJ: Lawrence Erlbaum.

Reys, R. E. (1984). Mental computation: Past, present and future. *Elementary School Journal, 84,* 547-557.

Schoenfeld, A. H. (1985). *Mathematical problem solving.* Orlando, FL: Academic Press.

Schoenfeld, A. H. (1987). Cognitive science and mathematics education: An overview. In A. H. Schoenfeld (Ed.), *Cognitive science and mathematics education* (pp. 1-32). Hillsdale, NJ: Lawrence Erlbaum.

Schoenfeld, A. H. (1989). Explorations of students' mathematical beliefs and behavior. *Journal for Research in Mathematics Education, 20,* 338-355.

Schwartz, J. L. (1989). Intensive quantity and referent transforming arithmetic operations. In J. Hiebert & M. Behr (Eds.), *Number concepts and operations in the middle grades* (pp. 41-52). Hillsdale, NJ: Lawrence Erlbaum.

Senk, S. L. (1989). Toward school algebra in the year 2000. In S. Wagner & C. Kieran (Eds.), *Research issues in the learning and teaching of algebra* (pp. 214-219). Hillsdale, NJ: Lawrence Erlbaum.

Silver, E. A. (1987). Foundations of cognitive theory and research for mathematics problem-solving. In A. H. Schoenfeld (Ed.), *Cognitive science and mathematics education* (pp. 33-60). Hillsdale, NJ: Lawrence Erlbaum.

Skemp, R. (1987). *The psychology of learning mathematics* (expanded U.S. ed.). Hillsdale, NJ: Lawrence Erlbaum.

Sowder, J. T. (1989). Mental computation and number comparison: Their roles in the development of number sense and computational estimation. In J. Hiebert & M. Behr (Eds.), *Number concepts and operations in the middle grades* (pp. 182-197). Hillsdale, NJ: Lawrence Erlbaum.

Stanic, G. M. A., & Kilpatrick, J. (1988). Historical perspectives on problem solving in the mathematics curriculum. In R. I. Charles & E. A. Silver

(Eds.), *The teaching and assessing of mathematical problem solving* (pp. 1-22). Hillsdale, NJ: Lawrence Erlbaum.

Steffe, L. P. (1989). Children's construction of number sequences and multiplying schemes. In J. Hiebert & M. Behr (Eds.), *Number concepts and operations in the middle grades* (pp. 119-140). Hillsdale, NJ: Lawrence Erlbaum.

Steffe, L. P., von Glasserfeld, E., Richards, J., & Cobb, P. (1983). *Children's counting types: Philosophy, theory and application.* New York: Praeger.

Stigler, J. W., & Perry, M. (1988). Cross-cultural studies of mathematics teaching and learning: Recent findings and new directions. In D. A. Grouws, T. J. Cooney, & D. Jones (Eds.), *Effective mathematics teaching* (pp. 194-223). Hillsdale, NJ: Lawrence Erlbaum.

Thorpe, J. (1989). Algebra: What should we teach and how should we teach it? In S. Wagner & C. Kieran (Eds.), *Research issues in the learning and teaching of algebra* (pp. 11-24). Hillsdale, NJ: Lawrence Erlbaum.

Usiskin, A. (1986). Reasons for estimating. In H. L. Schoen & M. J. Zweng (Eds.), *Estimation and mental computation* (pp. 1-15). Reston, VA: National Council of Teachers of Mathematics.

Vergnaud, G. (1989). Multiplicative structures. In J. Hiebert & M. Behr (Eds.), *Number concepts and operations in the middle grades* (pp. 141-161). Hillsdale, NJ: Lawrence Erlbaum.

Wearne, D., & Hiebert, J. (1989). Constructing and using meaning for mathematical symbols: The case of decimal fractions. In J. Hiebert & M. Behr (Eds.), *Number concepts and operations in the middle grades* (pp. 220-235). Hillsdale, NJ: Lawrence Erlbaum.

Wegner, R. H. (1987). Cognitive science and algebra learning. In A. H. Schoenfeld (Ed.), *Cognitive science and mathematics education* (pp. 217-252). Hillsdale, NJ: Lawrence Erlbaum.

Teaching

Ball, D. L. (1989, February). Teaching mathematics for understanding: What do teachers need to know about subject matter? In *Proceedings of National Center for Research in Teacher Education* (pp. 79-100). East Lansing, MI: National Center for Research on Teacher Education. (ERIC Document Reproduction Service No. ED 323 165)

Bauersfeld, H. (1988). Interaction, construction, and knowledge: Alternative perspectives for mathematics education. In D. A. Grouws, T. J. Cooney, & D. Jones (Eds.), *Effective mathematics teaching* (pp. 27-46). Hillsdale, NJ: Lawrence Erlbaum.

Bell, M., Esty, E., Payne, J. N., & Suydam, M. N. (1977). Hand-held calculators: Past, present, and future. In F. J. Crosswhite & R. E. Reys (Eds.), *Organizing for mathematics instruction* (pp. 224-240). Reston, VA: National Council of Teachers of Mathematics.

Berliner, D. C., Stein, P., Sabers, D., Clarridge, P. B., Cushing, K., & Pinnegar, S. (1988). Implications of research on pedagogical expertise and experience for mathematics teaching. In D. A. Grouws, T. J. Cooney, & D. Jones (Eds.), *Effective mathematics teaching* (pp. 67-95). Hillsdale, NJ: Lawrence Erlbaum.

Booth, L. R. (1989a). A question of structure. In S. Wagner & C. Kieran (Eds.), *Research issues in the learning and teaching of algebra* (pp. 57-59). Hillsdale, NJ: Lawrence Erlbaum.

Booth, L. R. (1989b). The research agenda in algebra: A mathematics education perspective. In S. Wagner & C. Kieran (Eds.), *Research issues in the learning and teaching of algebra* (pp. 238-246). Hillsdale, NJ: Lawrence Erlbaum.

Campione, J. C., Brown, A. L., & Connell, M. L. (1988). Metacognition: On the importance of understanding what you are doing. In R. I. Charles & E. A. Silver (Eds.), *The teaching and assessing of mathematical problem solving* (pp. 93-114). Hillsdale, NJ: Lawrence Erlbaum.

Carpenter, T. P. (1988). Teaching as problem solving. In R. I. Charles & E. A. Silver (Eds.), *The teaching and assessing of mathematical problem solving* (pp. 187-202). Hillsdale, NJ: Lawrence Erlbaum.

Case, R., & Sandieson, R. (1989). A developmental approach to the identification and teaching of central conceptual structures in mathematics and science in the middle grades. In J. Hiebert & M. Behr (Eds.), *Number concepts and operations in the middle grades* (pp. 236-259). Hillsdale, NJ: Lawrence Erlbaum.

Charles, R. I. (1988). Teacher education and mathematical problem solving: Some issues and directions. In R. I. Charles & E. A. Silver (Eds.), *The teaching and assessing of mathematical problem solving* (pp. 259-272). Hillsdale, NJ: Lawrence Erlbaum.

Cooney, T. J. (1981). Teachers' decision making. In E. Fennema (Ed.), *Mathematics education research: Implications for the '80s* (pp. 67-81). Alexandria, VA: Association for Supervision and Curriculum Development.

Cooney, T. J., Grouws, D. A., & Jones, D. (1986). An agenda for research on teaching mathematics. In D. A. Grouws, T. J. Cooney, & D. Jones (Eds.), *Effective mathematics teaching* (pp. 253-262). Hillsdale, NJ: Lawrence Erlbaum.

Crosswhite, F. J. (1987). Cognitive science and mathematics education: A mathematics educator's perspective. In A. H. Schoenfeld (Ed.), *Cognitive science and mathematics education* (pp. 265-278). Hillsdale, NJ: Lawrence Erlbaum.

Dessart, D. J. (1983). *Classroom ideas from research on secondary school mathematics.* Reston, VA: National Council of Teachers of Mathematics.

DeVault, M. (1981). Computers. In E. Fennema (Ed.), *Mathematics education research: Implications for the '80s* (pp. 131-148). Alexandria, VA: Association for Supervision and Curriculum Development.

Fisher, L. (1988). Strategies used by secondary mathematics teachers to solve proportion problems. *Journal for Research in Mathematics Education, 19,* 157-168.

Good, T. L., & Biddle, B. J. (1988). Research and the improvement of mathematics instruction: The need for observational resources. In D. A. Grouws, T. J. Cooney, & D. Jones (Eds.), *Effective mathematics teaching* (pp. 114-142). Hillsdale, NJ: Lawrence Erlbaum.

Good, T. L., & Grouws, D. A. (1981). Process-product research. In E. Fennema (Ed.), *Mathematics education research: Implications for the '80s* (pp. 82-91). Alexandria, VA: Association for Supervision and Curriculum Development.

Good, T. L., Grouws, D. A., & Ebmeier, H. (1983). *Active mathematics teaching.* New York: Longman.

Greeno, J. G. (1987). Instructional representations based on research about understanding. In A. H. Schoenfeld (Ed.), *Cognitive science and mathematics education* (pp. 61-88). Hillsdale, NJ: Lawrence Erlbaum.

Harrison, B., Brindley, S., & Bye, M. P. (1989). Allowing for student cognitive levels in the teaching of fractions and ratios. *Journal for Research in Mathematics Education, 20,* 288-300.

Henderson, A. (1987). From the teacher's side of the desk. In A. H. Schoenfeld (Ed.), *Cognitive science and mathematics education* (pp. 149-164). Hillsdale, NJ: Lawrence Erlbaum.

Herscovics, N. (1989). Cognitive obstacles encountered in the learning of algebra. In S. Wagner & C. Kieran (Eds.), *Research issues in the learning and teaching of algebra* (pp. 60-86). Hillsdale, NJ: Lawrence Erlbaum.

Hope, J. A., & Sherrill, J. M. (1987). Characteristics of unskilled and skilled mental calculators. *Journal for Research in Mathematics Education, 18,* 98-111.

Hoyles, C. (1988). From fragmentation to synthesis: An integrated approach to research on the teaching of mathematics. In D. A. Grouws, T. J. Cooney, & D. Jones (Eds.), *Effective mathematics teaching* (pp. 143-168). Hillsdale, NJ: Lawrence Erlbaum.

Kaput, J. J. (1989). Linking representations in the symbol systems of algebra. In S. Wagner & C. Kieran (Eds.), *Research issues in the learning and teaching of algebra* (pp. 167-194). Hillsdale, NJ: Lawrence Erlbaum.

Kennedy, L. M. (1984). *Guiding children's learning of mathematics.* Belmont, CA: Wadsworth.

Kieran, C. (1989). The early learning of algebra: A structural perspective. In S. Wagner & C. Kieran (Eds.), *Research issues in the learning and teaching of algebra* (pp. 33-56). Hillsdale, NJ: Lawrence Erlbaum.

Kirshner, D. (1989). Critical issues in current representation system theory. In S. Wagner & C. Kieran (Eds.), *Research issues in the learning and teaching of algebra* (pp. 195-198). Hillsdale, NJ: Lawrence Erlbaum.

Larkin, J. H. (1989). Robust performance in algebra: The role of the problem representation. In S. Wagner & C. Kieran (Eds.), *Research issues in the learning and teaching of algebra* (pp. 120-134). Hillsdale, NJ: Lawrence Erlbaum.

Lave, J., Smith, S., & Butler, M. (1988). Problem solving as everyday practice. In R. I. Charles & E. A. Silver (Eds.), *The teaching and assessing of mathematical problem solving* (pp. 61-81). Hillsdale, NJ: Lawrence Erlbaum.

Leinhardt, G. (1988). Expertise in instructional lessons: An example from fractions. In D. A. Grouws, T. J. Cooney, & D. Jones (Eds.), *Effective mathematics teaching* (pp. 47-66). Hillsdale, NJ: Lawrence Erlbaum.

Leitzel, J. R. (1989). Critical considerations for the future of algebra instruction. In S. Wagner & C. Kieran (Eds.), *Research issues in the learning and teaching of algebra* (pp. 25-32). Hillsdale, NJ: Lawrence Erlbaum.

Lester, F. K., Jr. (1988). Reflections about mathematical problem-solving research. In R. I. Charles & E. A. Silver (Eds.), *The teaching and assessing of mathematical problem solving* (pp. 115-124). Hillsdale, NJ: Lawrence Erlbaum.

Lewis, M. W. (1989). Intelligent tutoring systems: First steps and future directions. In S. Wagner & C. Kieran (Eds.), *Research issues in the learning and teaching of algebra* (pp. 162-166). Hillsdale, NJ: Lawrence Erlbaum.

National Council of Teachers of Mathematics. (1991). *Professional standards for teaching mathematics.* Reston, VA: Author.

Nickson, M. (1988). Pervasive themes and some departure points for research into effective mathematics teaching. In D. A. Grouws, T. J. Cooney, & D. Jones (Eds.), *Effective mathematics teaching* (pp. 245-252). Hillsdale, NJ: Lawrence Erlbaum.

Noddings, N. (1985). Small groups as a setting for research on mathematical problem solving. In E. A. Silver (Ed.), *Teaching and learning mathematical problem solving: Multiple research perspectives* (pp. 345-359). Hillsdale, NJ: Lawrence Erlbaum.

Noddings, N. (1988). Preparing teachers to teach mathematical problem solving. In R. I. Charles & E. A. Silver (Eds.), *The teaching and assessing of mathematical problem solving* (pp. 244-258). Hillsdale, NJ: Lawrence Erlbaum.

Peterson, P. L. (1989). Teaching for higher-order thinking in mathematics: The challenge for the next decade. In D. A. Grouws, T. J. Cooney, & D. Jones (Eds.), *Effective mathematics teaching* (pp. 2-26). Hillsdale, NJ: Lawrence Erlbaum.

Phillips, E. R., & Uprichard, A. E. (1989). Preparing elementary teachers to teach mathematics. In *Proceedings of National Center for Research in Teacher Education* (pp. 101-122). East Lansing, MI: National Center for Research on Teacher Education. (ERIC Document Reproduction Service No. ED 323 165)

Rachlin, S. L. (1989). The research agenda in algebra: A curriculum perspective. In S. Wagner & C. Kieran (Eds.), *Research issues in the learning and teaching of algebra* (pp. 257-265). Hillsdale, NJ: Lawrence Erlbaum.

Raphael, D., & Wahlstrom, M. (1989). The influence of instructional aids on mathematics achievement. *Journal for Research in Mathematics Education, 20,* 173-190.

Reys, R. E., Suydam, M. N., & Lindquist, M. M. (1989). *Helping children learn mathematics.* Englewood Cliffs, NJ: Prentice-Hall.

Romberg, T. A. (1988). Can teachers be professionals? In D. A. Grouws, T. J. Cooney, & D. Jones (Eds.), *Effective mathematics teaching* (pp. 224-244). Hillsdale, NJ: Lawrence Erlbaum.

Romberg, T. A., & Carpenter, T. P. (1986). Research on teaching and learning mathematics: Two disciplines of scientific inquiry. In M. C. Wittrock (Ed.), *Handbook of research on teaching* (3rd ed., pp. 850-873). New York: Macmillan.

Schoenfeld, A. H. (1987a). Cognitive science and mathematics education: An overview. In A. H. Schoenfeld (Ed.), *Cognitive science and mathematics education* (pp. 1-32). Hillsdale, NJ: Lawrence Erlbaum.

Schoenfeld, A. H. (1987b). What's all the fuss about metacognition? In A. H. Schoenfeld (Ed.), *Cognitive science and mathematics education* (pp. 189-216). Hillsdale, NJ: Lawrence Erlbaum.

Schoenfeld, A. H. (1988). Problem solving in context(s). In R. I. Charles & E. A. Silver (Eds.), *The teaching and assessing of mathematical problem solving* (pp. 82-92). Hillsdale, NJ: Lawrence Erlbaum.

Schofield, J. W., & Verban, D. (1988). Computer usage in the teaching of mathematics: Issues that need answers. In D. A. Grouws, T. J. Cooney, & D. Jones (Eds.), *Effective mathematics teaching* (pp. 169-193). Hillsdale, NJ: Lawrence Erlbaum.

Schwartz, J. L. (1989). Intensive quantity and referent transforming arithmetic operations. In J. Hiebert & M. Behr (Eds.), *Number concepts and operations in the middle grades* (pp. 41-52). Hillsdale, NJ: Lawrence Erlbaum.

Silver, E. A. (Ed.). (1985). *Teaching and learning mathematical problem solving: Multiple research perspectives.* Hillsdale, NJ: Lawrence Erlbaum.

Silver, E. A. (1988). Teaching and assessing mathematical problem solving: Toward a research agenda. In R. I. Charles & E. A. Silver (Eds.), *The teaching and assessing of mathematical problem solving* (pp. 273-282). Hillsdale, NJ: Lawrence Erlbaum.

Skemp, R. (1987). *The psychology of learning mathematics* (expanded U.S. ed.). Hillsdale, NJ: Lawrence Erlbaum.

Sowder, J. T., & Wheeler, M. M. (1989). The development of concepts and strategies used in computational estimation. *Journal for Research in Mathematics Education, 20,* 130-146.

Sowder, L. (1988). Choosing operations in solving routine story problems. In R. I. Charles & E. A. Silver (Eds.), *The teaching and assessing of mathematical problem solving* (pp. 148-158). Hillsdale, NJ: Lawrence Erlbaum.

Steinberg, R. M. (1987). Instruction on derived facts strategies in addition and subtraction. *Journal for Research in Mathematics Education, 16,* 337-355.

Stiff, L. V. (1989). Effects of teaching strategy, relevant knowledge, and strategy length on learning a contrived mathematical concept. *Journal for Research in Mathematics Education, 20,* 227-241.

Stigler, J. W., & Perry, M. (1988). Cross-cultural studies of mathematics teaching and learning: Recent findings and new directions. In D. A. Grouws, T. J. Cooney, & D. Jones (Eds.), *Effective mathematics teaching* (pp. 194-223). Hillsdale, NJ: Lawrence Erlbaum.

Tall, D. (1989). Different cognitive obstacles in a technological paradigm. In S. Wagner & C. Kieran (Eds.), *Research issues in the learning and teaching of algebra* (pp. 87-92). Hillsdale, NJ: Lawrence Erlbaum.

Thompson, A. G. (1988). Learning to teach mathematical problem solving: Changes in teachers' conceptions and beliefs. In R. I. Charles & E. A. Silver (Eds.), *The teaching and assessing of mathematical problem solving* (pp. 232-243). Hillsdale, NJ: Lawrence Erlbaum.

Thompson, P. W. (1989). Artificial intelligence, advanced technology, and learning and teaching algebra. In S. Wagner & C. Kieran (Eds.), *Research issues in the learning and teaching of algebra* (pp. 135-161). Hillsdale, NJ: Lawrence Erlbaum.

Wagner, S., & Kieran, C. (Eds.). (1989). *Research issues in the learning and teaching of algebra.* Hillsdale, NJ: Lawrence Erlbaum.

Wheeler, D. (1989). Contexts for research on the teaching and learning of algebra. In S. Wagner & C. Kieran (Eds.), *Research issues in the learning and teaching of algebra* (pp. 278-287). Hillsdale, NJ: Lawrence Erlbaum.

Index